JONATHAN E. BONNETTE • MATT LOVELADY • JOHN WASHENKO • SKYLER WITMAN

MONEY *momentum*

Research and editing: Mark Pittman
Cover design and book layout: Eric Parkinson

Second Edition
Published, marketed and distributed by WWLB, LLC.
ISBN 978-0-615-38344-6

Printed in the United States of America

TABLE OF CONTENTS

MONEY
momentum

CHAPTER ONE

BANKING SUCCESS STRATEGIES

"We hated the houses we could afford and couldn't afford the houses we loved. What's worse, most of the homes we could afford were fixer-uppers or needed the basements finished. I didn't have the extra money or the time to become a home renovator. We needed a livable home right away."

—Mark R.
Seattle, Wash.

Banking strategies have been successful for thousands of years. Even before the Egyptians formulated banking concepts, various types of banking methodologies existed. Some could argue that banking existed before the Assyrians invented assets as security and lent money to the money-changers. To a large extent, banking concepts have changed history and controlled the destiny of nations. Money has been lent, assets harnessed and increased, interest paid in and lent out again, exchange rates determined and amazing fortunes created.

The history of banking predates even the history of money. People used goods and services to trade for other goods and services. Grain and cattle were stored in temples and palaces — the most secure places at the time — with loans being made by temple priests to merchants. Even though these old banking systems have developed and improved for centuries, the basic concepts are universal and ageless. In fact, many banking processes were settled on and have thrived hidden from the masses. Wealth seems to shun intruders.

The concept of interest came from the idea of lending cattle. If you borrowed a herd of cattle for a year, you would be expected to return more than you borrowed because the herd would have multiplied over the course of the year.[1] If this was true of cattle, why shouldn't it be true of any other commodity borrowed? If you borrowed farming tools, you would be expected to return a portion of your crops along with the tools when the harvest was over. Tokens or markers were used to keep track of what was loaned. The simple approach of returning more than you borrowed is not only the key to opening the bank's vault, but it also has the potential to build your own wealth.

With the creation of written language, came the ability to record these transactions and calculations of interest. Alongside that recording ability brought debt. Lenders soon figured out that debt works unceasingly, day and night. Issuing debt quietly held the potential to grow wealth while helping others expand their business reach. Now merchants were working harder than ever to pay back what they owed to avoid penalties.

Before there was money, borrowers were literally paying for the inability to repay debt with their lives. The Code of Hammurabi, ca. 1790 B.C., outlined penalties for failure to repay debt:

> *"If any one fail to meet a claim for debt, and sell himself,*
> *his wife, his son, and daughter for money or give them*
> *away to forced labor: they shall work for three years in*
> *the house of the man who bought them, or the proprietor,*
> *and in the fourth year they shall be set free."* [2]

Control

Even before the creation of brick and mortar banks, lenders were called bankers. They quietly developed their trade of lending and discovered a means to enhance their new business called "banking." The open demand for their offering — merchants wanting to expand their business through debt — has virtually remained unchanged for thousands of years. The bankers of yesteryear held one dominant card close to their vest which was that debt allowed them to control the situation. Essentially, they could control lives by controlling the debt. Things haven't changed much for today's bankers or borrowers.

Although debt is now repaid with currency, don't we still earn that currency with our lives? We live in a society thriving on the practice of "buy now, pay later" — a limitless treasure trove for the bankers.

Do you know what the impact would be to purchasing a $20,000 vehicle if your income were $12.50 an hour? The answer is nearly an entire year's worth of your net wages*. So, do you wait a year to make that purchase while saving every penny you earn to buy the car? No. You still have to pay for your food, clothing, shelter, and other basic needs. Is it even possible to save every net cent you earn over the course of a year? Probably not. So, what do you do? Most of us would buy the car on credit and let a banker pay for the car — promising to repay, with interest, the money borrowed.

*	$12.50	*hourly wage*
x	2080	*annual work hours*
=	$26,000.00	*annual gross salary*
-	25%	*tax bracket*
=	$19,500.00	*net income*

Living life creates debt. Owning your own home, driving a well-maintained car, and pursuing a meaningful education cost money — money that must typically be borrowed from a financial institution. Banks carefully use specific strategies to make money and continue to be successful. While debt can assist you in enjoying life and pay for basic necessities, it can also wear out its welcome and wear down your desire to dream for a better tomorrow.

CHAPTER TWO

2

THE GREAT RECESSION

"It was the most embarrassing moment of my life. Even after it was auctioned off, we still owed money on a car we didn't have."

—Jake H.
Minneapolis, Minn.

Today's financial crisis began in 2007 and has earned the moniker "Great Recession" by many economists and the media. During the Great Recession, financial institutions have experienced many industry-shattering changes. Seemingly unsinkable giants — Lehman Brothers, Merrill Lynch, Wachovia, Washington Mutual and others — declared bankruptcy or were sold for pennies on the dollar. The Dow Jones Industrial Average dropped 53.78 percent from its all-time high on October 9, 2007, to its low on March 9, 2009.[3] Shares of huge companies like AIG, Sallie Mae and Citigroup lost from half to nearly all of their net worth.

The ripples of the Great Recession will be felt for decades. What caused this mind-boggling event? Partial blame can be placed on the mortgage crisis which clearly helped escalate the recession. It involved an investment tool known as mortgage-backed securities, wherein banks sold mortgages to other banks and investment firms.

When the housing market tanked, thousands of people found themselves with mortgage payments they couldn't afford. The number of debtors who defaulted on their loans soared. Real estate that was previously thought to be a secure asset no longer maintained its value. Banks couldn't make good on their debts so they were auctioned off in fire sales or fell into bankruptcy.[4]

The recession, which has extended internationally, has also been spurred along by other critical factors. During 2008, the price of energy (particularly gas and oil) fluctuated wildly. Food prices also jumped in 2008, reaching an all-time high during spring months.

In an attempt to bolster the failing economy, the federal government approved controversial bailout and stimulus packages. As of December 1, 2008, the government's financial rescue initiatives totaled an astonishing $8.5 trillion![5] The jury is still out on how effective the government's actions will be.

The New American Reality

While we don't know the long-term effects of America's sagging economy, one thing is certain — the Great Recession has created a new American reality. Consumer debt, foreclosure situations and bankruptcy rates are at all-time highs while savings accounts, investments and new business growth are at all-time lows.

As big businesses continue to collapse, it's clear the end of these turbulent times may be far off into the future. One telltale sign is soaring unemployment rates. In March 2010, the federal government reported that Michigan had the nation's highest unemployment rate at over 14 percent![6] Obviously, the failing automobile industry plays a significant factor in joblessness of the car manufacturing capital of the world.

Money Momentum

If there is any question about just how difficult times are, just turn on the evening news. You can't watch a single broadcast without being reminded about how America's economy is struggling. Stories about excessive government bailouts including the infamous "Car Allowance Rebate System (CARS)" program (aka "Cash for Clunkers") and million dollar bonuses for bank executives are among the most memorable.

But even into the third year of the Great Recession, headlines continue to focus on the economy. Will the housing market ever recover? When can we expect to see unemployment rates return to normal?

What Caused the Great Recession?

The specific causes of our economic devastation are not easily identified. As with any complex situation, the Great Recession can't be attributed to any single event. However, experts have identified a few key items that may have triggered the financial meltdown including too much debt among American families and businesses.

This terrible economic period has proven that we live in a culture that accepts and even encourages excessive credit — even when debt soars to unreasonably high levels. It seems that debt has become the new 'American Reality'. Proof is in the statistic that nearly 9,000 people seek some form of advice on debt every day.[7] As a result, debt counseling has become a $7 billion industry![8]

While debt seems to be continually creeping into the majority of American households, it is estimated that hundreds of thousands of individuals bear the burden of debt alone. Some experts believe that internalizing debt can be a silent killer because debt reaches into so many areas of our lives and personal health. In fact, the impact of debt is so strong that it was studied by the U.S. Air Force. The study that showed "… excessive indebtedness can become an impediment to dependable productivity and mission readiness."[9]

Instead of internalizing financial troubles, those individuals and their families struggling to repay their debts should make the conscious decision to change their financial situation. Many companies offer financial tools to help you make wise decisions about your personal finances, rid yourself and your family from the shackles of personal debt and gain financial independence.

No matter how small and seemingly insignificant, each of us contributed to our current economic meltdown. Now is the time for Americans to take responsibility for their actions and choose fiscal responsibility in place of consumer debt.

How Can You Protect Yourself?

Since the United States suffered its first recession, the panic of 1797, there have been at least 22 measured financial downturns, including the Great Depression. America has experienced 10 recessions since World War II, the average duration being 10.4 months.[10]

Recessions have occurred with disturbing regularity. The causes are varied, as are the end result. Although it is impossible to predict exactly what might happen as a result of an economic swing, here are just a few possibilities:

- **Loss of Employment**
- **Property values may decline**
- **IRA or stock portfolio may lose value**
- **Banks may fail**
- **Sources of capital may dry up**
- **Different parts of the economy may collapse**

The best way to protect yourself and your assets during these periods of economic difficulty is to have your financial house in order. Personal financial freedom occurs only when no claim can be made against your assets via debt. Complete debt elimination protects against the dangers inherent in a recession.

Avoid panic by controlling how and when your debts are paid off. By utilizing the system we have developed, you can strengthen and protect your financial well-being through the incorporation of the four pillars of financial freedom:

- **Debt Elimination**
- **Wealth Building**
- **Retirement Planning**
- **Legacy Planning**

"Since the United States suffered its first recession, the panic of 1797, there have been at least 22 measured financial downturns, including the Great Depression."

The Great Recession

THE EMOTION OF PERSONAL FINANCES

"I had put so much effort into surviving this ordeal, but nothing ever seemed to come of it. I wish I'd been more prepared for something like this. Even a few hundred dollars in the bank would have changed my entire situation when this all started."

—Rhonda L.
Dallas, Texas

While it's true that money cannot buy happiness, it often has a marked effect on virtually every facet of our lives. Personal finances affect your physical and mental health, your self-esteem and can extend into workplace relationships. Debt can affect an otherwise happy household and disrupt relationships with your significant other, children, extended family and even your friends.

But if money can't buy happiness, why do we allow it to have such a far-reaching effect in our lives? First, it's important to consider how prevalent money matters really are in America. Statistics show that the average adult spends 80 percent of their awake time on earning, spending or simply thinking about personal finances.[11] As a result, we spend more time devoted to money issues than anything else in our lives.

A Catalyst to Change

Money consumes most of our waking hours and has numerous emotional ramifications. Personal funds are often viewed as a vehicle to achieving our hopes and dreams, family expectations, self-worth, security, life experiences, and many other core feelings and beliefs. As a result, money and money management is often very emotional, making financial decisions an important part of our lives and our most endearing relationships.

When a couple works together to achieve financial goals, it positively influences the relationship. For example, one study among recently married couples showed that those who paid off their consumer debt over a period of five years reported being more satisfied with their marriage. Couples who paid off only a portion of their consumer debt or couples who assumed large amounts of debt during the same period reported decreased marital satisfaction.[12]

Spending to Self-Medicate

Money is also highly emotional because many Americans spend money as a coping mechanism for the challenges of daily life. Similar to overeating, experts believe that people use shopping to handle stress and feelings of disappointment, loneliness, insecurity, boredom, etc. According to one source, as many as 15 million Americans spend money as a direct response to stress and other emotions.[13]

Oftentimes this emotional band-aid shopping spree is paid for with plastic. People are not only willing to spend, but to spend significantly more when paying with credit instead of cash. Thus, self-medicated shopping usually results in overspending and compounds the stress load. Instead of using money as a tool to achieve a fulfilling life, these hyper-consumers use money to escape their everyday problems.

Money Momentum

Another emotional shopping habit is overspending in general. Some consumers regularly spend more than they make every single month. A new study in the *Journal of Consumer Research* shows that the problem may be the result of low self-esteem. Individuals who feel powerless often make expensive purchases and pay higher prices for products that convey high status. "It suggests that in contemporary America, people use consumer purchases to compensate for psychological states of insecurity," the study stated.[14]

Another insightful study was conducted among two groups found on the same bus route in India. The first group was exposed to bus accident injuries. The second group (found on the same route) was not exposed to the accident. Researchers discovered that spending was the primary way participants in the first group alleviated their shock. After time, those exposed to the accident maintained a significantly higher level of debt than those who were not exposed to the accident.[15]

A Lack of Fiscal Control

Another reason money is so emotional is because the majority of Americans don't have control of their personal finances. Consider these staggering financial statistics:

- 57% of households do not have a budget.[16]
- 20% of those earning $100,000 or more still live paycheck to paycheck.[16]
- 70% of Americans live paycheck to paycheck.[17]
- 25% of Americans believe they are well informed about managing their money.[17]
- 40% of families live off 110% of their income.[17]
- 64% of 18–24 year olds don't know the interest rate on their credit cards.[17]

Poorly managed personal finances and consumer debt create a tremendous amount of stress for the entire family. If everyday expenses aren't kept in check, it generates increased strain among family members (particularly spouses) when the bills arrive. Unable to be paid, bills are often tucked away in a drawer and ignored. In fact, almost 25 percent of American's don't even look at their monthly credit card statement.[18]

Avoidance doesn't stop the calls from creditors, and ignoring the calls only worsens an already stressful situation. Unfortunately, because the family is behind on their bills from the previous month, personal finances are now in greater disarray the following month. The cycle continues out of control indefinitely.

In denial, many people don't even realize how desperate their financial situations are until they simply can't maintain their false lifestyle anymore. One study found that 58 percent of respondents claimed that they paid off their credit cards in full each month. Yet national statistics show that only about 40 percent of card holders pay off the balance.[18] Researchers believe this discrepancy results from people lying to themselves about the reality of their personal finances.

Interestingly, many people really don't understand just how poorly they manage their money. Although 57 percent of Americans don't have a household budget, most financial management experts believe that a budget is the first step in gaining control of personal finances and building wealth. According to a counselor at the American Credit Counseling Service, approximately 80 percent of financial hardship stems from simply living beyond your means — something a household budget helps control.[19]

Money Momentum

MONEY MANAGEMENT SKILLS

*"It was the last thing I expected for my retirement —
getting a job. I wanted to kick back and enjoy life. Instead,
I was working 40 hours a week — just like I was before."*

**—Herb F.
Portage, Ind.**

A substantial amount of research has been conducted on how Americans manage their personal finances. Often, the success or failure of an individual's personal finances is attributed to the *locus of control*. This psychological term refers to a belief about what causes good or bad things to happen in life and how much the individual can control these events. Individuals with high levels of *internal* locus of control believe that life events result from their own actions and behaviors. Those with a high level of *external* locus of control assume that their environment, a higher power, the government, other people, fate, chance, etc., determine life events.[20]

In personal finances, individuals with external locus of control often have poor money management skills and correspondingly high levels of debt. In contrast, those with internal locus of control often have better money management skills. The concept of locus of control also helps explain additional research findings: Individuals with higher self-esteem, stress management strategies and personal motivation tend to have better financial circumstances. In contrast, poor financial skills coincide with lower self-esteem, poor stress management skills and weak self-efficacy skills. In other words, these people are less willing to perform behaviors required to achieve goals and persist in the face of adversity.[21]

Money and Your Relationship

It has become a well-known fact that money is one of, if not the greatest, influence on a relationship — especially a marriage. The current divorce rate is at a staggering 51 percent. Why? Approximately 80–90 percent of those failed marriages blame financial problems as the cause of their divorce.[22] Finances are also cited as the most common point of disagreement among couples who remain married. Yet many of these "successful" marriages have reduced levels of marital fulfillment and satisfaction because of finances.

Why is Money So Controversial in Marriage?

There are many reasons that financial conflict is so prevalent in marriage. First, money and spending has many emotional ties. After all, funds are usually required to achieve your hopes and dreams. Money helps determine a family's lifestyle and experiences, security, and even its overall identity. Finances are also an easy point of conflict because few individuals choose to spend their money in exactly the same way as their partner. As a result, arguments about finances are usually more intense and more negative than other disagreements.

In addition, money is one of the few resources in a relationship that can be exploited unilaterally. When this occurs, one party in the relationship has the ability to make financial decisions by himself/herself that can dramatically change the financial picture of the couple and the entire family — sometimes for the rest of their lives. Oftentimes the other spouse sees this form of single-party spending as a significant breach of trust. This irresponsible use of family funds is a difficult challenge for couples to overcome. In some cases, it is even more destabilizing to the marriage than a sexual affair.[23]

Another reason money can be so controversial is its time implications. Again, it is estimated that American adults spend 80 percent of their time earning, spending or thinking about money.[24] In this instance, time literally means money. After all, time and energy spent on obtaining money means time away from your spouse or significant other. Or when one member of the marriage partnership chooses to spend money, it may mean that he/she puts a higher priority on the material possession than on spending time with their spouse.

The Influence of Money

A 2006 study about personal finances revealed some informative facts about the tie between money and happiness in a marriage. Here are some of the study's findings:

- 23% of adults admitted that money problems adversely affected personal relationships.
- 37% of adults spend less quality time with their spouse as a result of money woes.
- 50% have more arguments and a shorter temper when worried about personal finances.
- 19% of participants even admitted to a loss of sexual libido because of money worries.

While the management of money takes a toll on most couples, the mismanagement of funds and the addition of debt can ruin a marriage. Two-thirds of Americans feel that debt is one of the top five deterrents in achieving a fulfilling relationship. In addition, most couples who characterize their marriage as happy and satisfying, do not engage in major debt.[24] One reason for the findings may be that patient couples who are working together to achieve family goals are more willing to delay a purchase until they have the funds available to pay cash for it. Obviously, patience and similar values/goals among both parties are an important factor in any successful marriage.

The Crushing Blow of Debt on Newlyweds

Debt is particularly prevalent among newlyweds because bringing debt into a marriage is one of the biggest causes of marital problems. Approximately 67 percent of women and 74 percent of men enter marriage with at least some debt including credit cards, car loans, student loans, medicals bills and other forms of consumer-related debt. About half of those who carry debt into the marriage owe more than $5,000.[24] To make matters worse, many individuals enter marriage without telling their partner about all of their financial obligations.[23]

Assumed debt from a spouse may be particularly harmful because both parties didn't have a say in the accumulation of the debt.[25] Financial obligations for newlyweds are particularly dangerous because the first few years of marriage are the most vulnerable. Some 20 percent of divorces in the United States occur within the first five years of marriage.[24] In correlation,

"Many studies have found that personal finance management skills are best taught at home."

Money Momentum

during the first few years of marriage, couples usually experience tight budgets, high debts and expenses. All this extreme financial strain is also occurring during the first phases of their careers and building a family. Instead of focusing on establishing a good marriage and goals for the future, the couple is forced to solve financial problems.

The Impact of Finances on Your Family

Financial troubles at home don't just negatively affect the relationship with your spouse. Unfortunately, the mismanagement of funds by adults hurts children as well. More than one in four adults who allow finances to adversely affect their relationships admit that money worries make them spend less quality time with their children. In addition, when money is tight, tempers flare, creating a negative environment for everyone in the home — especially the children.[26]

Psychologists believe that economic hardships in the family dramatically affect children. They cite perceptions of economic pressure by the children, weakening family relationships, and disruptive parenting practices as consequences of financial hardship.[27] One study shows that economic hardship indirectly affects the self-esteem of early adolescents due to decreased parental support and involvement.[28]

If a family experiences a financial crisis, high school students may be required to seek part-time employment to help support the family. Studies also show that a teenager's time working an after-school job diminishes time spent with family, not time spent with friends.

In summary, poor financial management and excessive debt limits the options of the entire family. If your household is in debt or lacks savings, you may be forced to stay working at a bad job. Relocating, even to a better paying job, is often not an option. Debt also means time away from your spouse and children, working off the principal and interest payments, again weakening essential family ties. Furthermore, the mismanagement of funds increases arguments between spouses, many times in front of children. The children ultimately suffer the most stress because they worry about their parents' relationship, and can even place blame onto themselves.

Teaching Financial Skills

Many studies have found that personal finance management skills are best taught at home. Typically, the spending (or savings) patterns of adults are passed on to their children. This might be a startling trend considering that only 25 percent of Americans feel that they are well informed about managing their money. A similarly small amount of parents feel equipped to teach their children about money. A whopping 50 percent of parents admit they don't set a good example for their children in the area of personal finances.[30]

A recent survey showed that 70 percent of parents claim to have talked to their teens about the dangers of credit cards. Yet only 44 percent of the teens of these respondents believe their parents have discussed credit with them. So if parents aren't teaching their children effective money management skills, where is the next generation going to learn these essential, life-long beneficial skills? What's worse is that only seven states teach some financial management skills in school.[30] In short, they aren't being taught financial lessons at all. These children will end up earning money long before they understand how to manage it.

Another concern is that money management skills are needed at an earlier age than ever before. Many marketers have started focusing their advertising dollars on the 'tween market (children 8–12 years old) because of their expansive purchasing power. Unfortunately, most 'tweens, teens and young adults are never taught how to manage their funds until it's too late. No one is teaching them about the dangers of credit card debt. As a result, young adults are getting into financial trouble right out of high school (or even sooner).

One study, conducted in 1998, showed that 80 percent of college students have at least one credit card. Over the last decade, that number has climbed as American spending and debt has spiraled out of control. Without financial education or experience, young adults are making poor financial decisions. [30]

We live in a society of pro-credit, instead of anti-debt. From an early age, children are taught by their parents that spending and consumerism can buy happiness. Yet at some point, the spending has to be controlled. America's current economic recession has taught us that to financially overextend ourselves, our families, our businesses and our nation will only result in financial woes. Once we learn to control our spending and make educated financial decisions, we need to pass those hard-learned lessons onto our children to create a more fiscally aware and responsible America.

The Effects of Poverty

It's easy to see how fiscal irresponsibility and excessive debt can lead to financial bondage. But if excessive consumption isn't controlled, the mismanagement of funds can easily lead to poverty. Even families with high incomes can become impoverished when they carry extremely high debt-to-income ratios. High debt payments can leave little money left over for necessities of life such as food, clothing and shelter.

Most likely because of the media, we are well aware of the extreme poverty in countries around the world. But unfortunately, many American families live in poverty right in your hometown — even in your own neighborhood. The effects of poverty on families, especially children, are catastrophic. Children born into poverty are more likely to have a low birth weight, high infant mortality and poor general health. Because high-quality foods often cost more, these children have meager diets that lack proper nutrition and do not adequately support their physical and mental needs.

Housing is also a significant concern among the impoverished. The poor often live in low-income housing that is normally subsidized by the federal government. These dwellings are often overcrowded, dirty and even damp. This increases the likelihood of contracting infectious diseases and respiratory conditions such as asthma and allergies. In addition, both children and adults who live in low-income housing often have excessive stress, usually derived from inadequate personal finances.

There is also a correlation between childhood accidents and the scarcity of funds. Poor children are 15 times more likely to die in a fire at home and three times more likely to be hit by a car than children from higher income families. Even burn victim rates are significantly higher among poor children.[31] There are a wide variety of factors that explain these statistics. Oftentimes impoverished families only have one parent in the home running the entire household, and that parent spends a significant amount of time at work trying to provide the bare necessities of life. As a result, children may become latchkey kids and be left unsupervised for extended periods of time. In addition, long work hours lead to tired and over-worked parents who are inattentive to their children when they arrive home.

Poverty extends more forcefully into the lives of teens. Teenage girls who come from households in the lowest income bracket are 10 times more likely to become a teenage mother than girls who come from the highest income bracket. The death rate for babies of teenage mothers is 60 percent higher than other infants. Also, students who receive subsidized lunches at school because they come from a low-income home are more likely to start smoking cigarettes than other students. [31]

Money Momentum

CHAPTER FIVE CHAPTER FIVE

5

PERSONAL FINANCES AND YOUR HEALTH

"It took a while to get it through my thick head that easy credit quickly turns into chasing interest charges for the rest of your life."

—Kiri H.
Minneapolis, Minn.

R egardless of your sex, age, income or marital status, your personal finances play an important role in your health. Individuals who manage their money well are less likely to be physically influenced by finance-related stresses. However, individuals with poor money management skills, particularly those who carry high levels of debt, are often physically, emotionally and mentally drained by their financial burdens.

Numerous studies have been conducted on the correlation between health and personal finances. According to one study, 20 percent of adults were physically affected simply by the mere thought of personal finances. In addition, 45 percent of respondents felt anxiety, 15 percent felt immobilized and 12 percent felt physically ill.[32]

Chronic Stress

Probably the most common way that money can influence your health is stress. According to the American Psychological Association, 73 percent of Americans listed money as the number one stress factor in their life. Ordinary stress can be managed by your body's natural defense systems. When induced, the stress hormones cortisol and adrenaline are released into the body. These hormones increase your heart rate, blood pressure, breathing, muscle tension, inflammation, etc. Every time you "feel" stress, your body is employing these survival tactics.[33]

Stress hormones are a remarkable part of the body's natural ability to survive in case of an emergency. However, it isn't healthy to employ your body's physical emergency response system every time you look at your bank account or sort through the bills. Because your body is working hard to cope with high levels of stress, it has diminished resources to fight infection, disease or even the common cold. As a result, you are more susceptible to illness. Doctor bills and prescription costs only increase financial difficulties. On the other hand, some people deal with their financial stress through dangerous "treatment" methods such as drugs, alcohol, smoking, overeating, etc.

If unable to pay your financial obligations, your mind will consider these bills to be a threat, turning your money woes into chronic stress. The situation is even worse if you don't have an accurate picture of your finances. You will constantly worry about the situation without having all

"If unable to pay your financial obligations, your mind will consider these bills to be a threat, turning your money woes into chronic stress."

Money Momentum

of the facts. Incomplete information often leads to playing out the worse situation in your mind, stimulating the body's natural response to stress. Approximately 25 percent of the working population misses an average of 16 days of work every year due to chronic stress.[34] Missed work means a decreased paycheck and even the potential to be fired, making the financial strain even worse.

Mental Health

Anxiety over finances also leads to depression, grief, despair, psychological disorders and insomnia. The Forum for Mental Health reported more than 50 percent of those in debt have some form of mental health concern. In contrast, only 14 percent of those not in debt suffered from mental health problems. In addition, those who owe money to five or more creditors are six times more likely to have these health problems.

The report continued to provide information about the physical benefits of getting out of debt. Approximately 85 percent of those in debt and suffering mental health problems saw significant improvement to their health within four years of seeking help with their finances. This data confirms that ignoring debt only aggravates the situation.[35]

Suicide

Tragically, financial enslavement has even pushed individuals to contemplate taking their own life and even following through with suicide. A study of court death files was conducted to examine the influence of debt on suicide victims. Suicide rates among men from 25 to 39 years old has increased 70 percent since 1997.[36] The increase may be due to the fact that men often feel financially responsible for their families. In addition, this age group earns a lower income then older, more established colleagues. Notwithstanding, the younger demographic usually has higher expenses than his older colleagues that stem from raising a family.

James Scurlock created a documentary titled Maxed Out. The film features the families of two college students who killed themselves due to credit card debt. "All the people we talked to had considered suicide at least once," Scurlock told a gathering of the National Association of Consumer Bankruptcy Attorneys in 2007. According to the Los Angeles Times, lawyers in the audience described "clients who showed up at their offices with cyanide or threatened, 'If you don't help me, I've got a gun in my car.'"

Sadly, using suicide as a way to escape debt seems to be an international phenomenon. An estimated 150,000 indebted Indian farmers have chosen to commit suicide since 1997.[37] As consumers, we need to carefully consider the consequences that debt has on our lives. In some situations, people are choosing to get so far in debt that they see suicide as the only way out. What a catastrophic waste of human life — all due to the mismanagement of money.

Our Current Economic State

- *50% of Americans have less than one month of savings.[38]*
- *56% of people do not know that credit score is the most important factor when applying for a loan.[38]*
- *57% of households do not have a budget.[38]*
- *61% of Americans are living paycheck to paycheck.[38]*
- *One in five of those earning $100,000 are living paycheck to paycheck.[38]*
- *In 2008, American credit card debt reached $972.73 billion.[38]*
- *Average credit card debt per household was $8,329.[38]*
- *Approximately 40% of families live off 110% of their incomes.[39]*
- *In 2006 (even before the Great Recession), personal savings rates dipped to negative 1.5%.[39]*
- *40% of Americans will never have a net worth of more than $10,000.[40]*

Money Momentum

OTHER WAYS YOUR MONEY AFFECTS YOU

"At first, I didn't think much of the so-called "Great Recession." Every economy has its ups and downs. Kind of like taking one step back and two steps forward. But when I began noticing friends and business associates getting laid off and struggling financially, I started to worry."

—Mark R.
Seattle, Wash.

Financial woes can affect personality and temperament because it causes feelings of anger, embarrassment and shame. These feelings affect the debtor and those who fall within their sphere of influence — particularly the family. Consumers may feel fear, frustration and unhappiness when they cannot repay their debts and creditors begin calling. They also have uncertainty about what the future holds for themselves and their families.

Optimism Bias

One psychologist believes that individuals are prone to "optimism bias." Under this theory, people believe that their situation is actually better than it is. Optimism bias is easily applied to personal finances. Consumers believe that their finances are better than they actually are until they can no longer deny the reality of their situation. Afterwards, feelings of anger and resentment set in.

Perhaps because of the theory of optimism bias, many consumers don't realize how desperate their finances have become until they are thousands of dollars in debt with no way to repay the funds. Many consumers deny that their personal finances are in ruin. In fact, only one in four adults can accurately state how much money they owe on outstanding loans. One in 10 adults have no idea how much debt they have accumulated![42]

The Consequences of Poor Money Management

Other examples of the dramatic influences of debt and fiscal mismanagement are evictions, bankruptcies, foreclosures, lawsuits and wage garnishments. The foreclosure rate in 2009 hit record highs at 2.82 million residential properties (21 percent increase over 2008). That figure doesn't include foreclosures among second homes, land parcels and business properties.[43] In the third quarter of 2009 alone, 937,840 properties had some form of foreclosure action taken against the property. That means that one in every 136 homes received a foreclosure notice.[44] Bankruptcy rates also soared. During 2009, nearly 1.5 million bankruptcies were filed (35 percent increase over 2008).[45]

Foreclosures and bankruptcies might be extreme for some Americans. But the lack of appropriate funds influences your daily life, too. Credit becomes particularly important when trying to purchase a new car or home because your credit score is the most important factor when applying for a loan. Thirty percent of your credit score is based on how much debt you carry (debt-to-credit limit ratio). Your credit score also determines what interest rate will be tied to your loan.

FICO Credit Score

Did you know there is a significant difference in how much money you will pay if you have a 670 FICO score versus a 760 FICO score? The difference usually means almost two-thirds of a percentage point. On a $200,000 home with a 30-year mortgage, that translates into almost $28,000 in extra interest payments.[46] Your credit score also influences the interest rates on your credit cards. Statistics regarding average American credit card debt varies dramatically, depending on the source. But various studies show that average credit card debt is somewhere between $8,000 and $15,000 per household. According to industry research group CardWeb.com, the average American with a credit card owes $8,523 in credit card debt. At an average APR of 14.4 percent, that translates into paying as much as $1,100 per year in interest payments alone.[47]

The Education Angle

In today's society, it's a well-known fact that higher education increases your annual earning potential. In 2009, high school dropouts averaged only $23,608 per year. Those who graduated from high school made an average of $32,552 annually. Some college education, but not a bachelor's degree, afforded the typical working American $37,752 annually. Those with a college degree made an average of $53,300 annually (that's a 41 percent increase over just having some college education). Next, an advanced degree meant an average of $69,056 annually for your family. Those with professional degrees such as doctors, lawyers and dentists earn an average of $99,300 annually.[48] It's easy to see how additional education, at any level, can make a substantial financial impact on your life and the lives of your family members.

Unemployment

Education also plays an important role in unemployment rates. The latest research, published in February 2010, shows how important education is in regards to unemployment. Job shortages have been a great problem in America throughout the Great Recession, attracting significant attention from the government and the media. In early 2010, national unemployment rates were above 10 percent.

However, your susceptibility to unemployment depends on your level of education. For those without a high school diploma, unemployment rates reached 15.6 percent. However, individuals with a bachelor's degree or higher enjoyed an unemployment rate that's one-half the national average at 5 percent.[48] The lesson? Education is a critical part of achieving financial independence for yourself and your family.

The Barriers of Education

Most people with money problems stemming from poverty, excessive debt or lack of savings desperately want to escape their financial burdens and corresponding lifestyle. Achieving higher education seems to be a logical step in the right direction. After all, 72 percent of America's poorest men and 67 percent of America's poorest women either dropped out of high school or only have a high school diploma.[49]

While education seems to be the simple answer, it is extremely difficult for those with extreme financial hardship to escape the trap of poverty. Research continues to show over and over again that higher education attainment means more income. But college rates among low-income earners have only slightly increased during the past three decades. In 2003, 8.6 percent of the nation's poorest young adults earned bachelor's degrees, barely up from 7.1 percent in 1975.[50]

The vast majority of individuals in poverty are so busy working at a low paying job they don't have time for obtaining additional education. Instead, they focus their time and efforts on picking up an extra shift or working a second or even third job just to put a meager meal on the table.
Money Momentum

Many poor Americans also lack the support system needed to successfully return to school. Many of their parents did not achieve higher education, and as a result they may not see the need (or maybe the practicality) of college when there are so many other demands in life. In addition, these parents can't provide any advice or tips on applying to school, obtaining funding (loans/grants), selecting a college, etc.

Other statistics show that only 53 percent of poor high school students were prepared for college compared to 86 percent of wealthy students.[50] In areas of the country where poverty is dominant, expectations are very low. Some schools are just trying to get their students to graduate from high school with no ambition for assisting in their future education. Drugs, teenage pregnancy, violence and other problems that are often correlated with poverty become the focus instead of higher education.

Another concern is funding higher education. College is a very expensive undertaking. A private college in 2009–2010 costs an average of $26,273 per year in tuition alone (approximately $100,000 for a bachelor's degree). The average cost of an in-state, public college is $7,020 per year (approximately $30,000 for a bachelor's degree).[48] In addition, students must consider the costs of living expenses, textbooks and general school supplies. Depending on the location of the school, transportation issues could also be a heavy financial burden on the student. While loans/grants and other funding are available, many first-generation students don't know where to apply or that help even exists.

Finally, it's important to consider attitude toward education. Many of America's poor families are struggling to survive and their children's education becomes a secondary priority. Educators believe that the home environment is the single most important factor in influencing educational outcomes.

Unfortunately, students from impoverished homes often struggle at school, beginning as early as elementary school. These students are more

Other Ways Your Money Affects You

"Many of America's poor families are struggling to survive and their children's education becomes a secondary priority."

likely to score lower on their achievement tests. They are twice as likely to repeat a grade, be expelled or suspended from school or drop out of school entirely. Poor students are also 1.4 times as likely to be identified as having a learning disability.[51] Plagued with low expectations from their teachers, administrators, parents, and even their family and peers, they have low expectations for themselves.

Familial economics have many impacts on student success. One study ranked 150 high schools based on average entrance exam scores. Students were divided into categories. G1 students had the highest entrance exams scores and G5 students had the lowest test scores. Those in the G1 group showed a 2.3 percent dropout rate while the G5 group had a 33 percent dropout rate. Nearly 90 percent of those in the G1 category lived in owner-occupied housing compared to 56 percent of those in the G5 category. The rest of the students lived in rental properties. Another telling statistic about the G5 group was food availability and consumption. Approximately 40 percent of G5 students were not given breakfast and 20 percent were not given dinner, a sign of extreme poverty.[52]

CHAPTER SEVEN

RECYCLING DEBT

"I work my fingers to the bone, I'm going to school, and I try really hard to find time to spend with my kids. But after all my extra effort, I wasn't any better off than I was before. I was in debt up to my neck and drowning."

—Rhonda L.
Dallas, Texas

All types of financial institutions that make money from money know all about instant gratification and impulse buying today's shoppers seem to be addicted to. They don't hesitate to use these powerful marketing tools to their fiscal advantage. Look around your home, how many items did you never intend to purchase but are now paying interest on? Too often, the heavy burden of debt management falls to the path of least resistance, which moves it around into an endless loop of recycling debt.

We live in a "me first" financial world. That's why today's financial crisis can, in part, be attributed to the lure of out-of-this-world bonuses on Wall Street and the commission-driven sales tactics of subprime lenders. When sales commissions are involved, the attraction of earning higher commissions for the same amount of effort creates an ever-widening rift that puts the needs of the consumer at odds with the intentions of the financial professional. No laws are broken, but greed can lead to bad judgment.

For some consumers, marketing campaigns and sales tactics direct the focus toward the extremely tempting lure of low minimum payments. Too often, the side effects of these "savings" skew the ability to understand the long-term impact. The gratification will be INSTANT, but, rest assured, it will wear off quickly. The "bill me later" plan agreed to so easily will arrive later in the form of DEBT.

Such debt comes in all shapes and sizes, including (but not limited to): mortgage debt, car loans, student loans, credit card debt, debt consolidation loans and the infamous payday loans. Some of these debts are necessary and even smart, but many are the product of excessive and unnecessary purchases or even acts of desperation. The end result is simply bad debt. We have all seen MasterCard's "Priceless" commercials with the slogan "There are some things money can't buy. For everything else, there's MasterCard." We have been conditioned to believe that going into debt for something you want is OK, it's "Priceless." But those purchases most definitely have a price and associated interest charges that quickly accumulate and can spiral out of control with a devastating impact on your financial health..

Unless you have cash put away to pay for big-ticket items, you are likely spending money you do not have. It's an easy step to go from bad debt to being forced to use credit to pay for basic necessities like food and rent. "A large credit balance used to be evidence of a shopping frenzy or luxurious trip. Now, we're paying the rent with plastic. Survival debt is a bad, bad sign." [53]

The False Positive of Refinancing

Oftentimes consumers choose to refinance their mortgage in an attempt to collateralize or "cash out" the equity in their home. In fact, due to historically low interest rates and increased consumer debt, refinancing in recent years has reached epidemic proportions. Refinancing can be seen as a remedy for financial woes. But is it really? The Federal Reserve Board warns that the monthly savings may not exceed the costs of refinancing. "It is not unusual to pay 3–6 percent of your outstanding principal in refinancing fees. These expenses are in addition to any prepayment penalties or other costs for paying off any mortgages you might have."[53]

In addition, refinancing restarts the amortization process. Early payments for most mortgages go chiefly to interest — a process called front-loading. Thus, refinancing essentially turns back the clock and most of your monthly payment goes to paying interest and not to building equity.[53] Promises of "no cost" refinancing are invariably deceiving. According to the Federal Reserve Board, they are accomplished in one of two ways:

1) The lender covers the closing costs but charges a higher interest rate *for the for the life of the loan.*
2) The refinancing fees are rolled into the loan and become part of the principal, which you will be repaying, with interest, *for the life of the loan.*[54]

If borrowers cashed out some of the equity in their home during refinancing, they undoubtedly went years, even decades, backwards in getting out of debt. In trading debt for debt (aka recycling debt), the refinancing (new debt) lifted little or none of the actual debt burden. In fact, it actually *increased* the burden! Often, the "extra savings" generated through the exercise of debt recycling results in a false positive — nothing more than the homeowner extending their debt payoff schedule. The end result? More years are required to pay off even more debt.

Subprime Lenders

In the case of borrowers with less than perfect credit, subprime lenders can seem like a way out of debt — the break the borrower had been praying for. In reality, a subprime loan can place the borrower in an even worse situation than they were in to begin with — in fact, much worse. Although subprime mortgage loans were meant to give people with blemished credit a second chance at homeownership, many borrowers were given loans they simply couldn't afford.

The worst subprime loans — called "No Documentation" loans — caused the most damage to the housing market. Although the borrower has the feeling of "qualifying" for the loan, the only required documentation was a valid Social Security Number (SSN), an adequate credit profile, a qualifying property and little to no proof of income. Not only does this mean the loan did not meet Fannie Mae or Freddie Mac underwriting guidelines, even a few credit dings could give the subprime lender the ability to significantly increase your interest rate.

The end result was the borrower accepting keys to homes they couldn't afford. In some cases, borrowers began their cycle of default by missing their very first payment. While the subprime lender chalked up another sale or refinance, the debt load rested squarely on the shoulders of the borrower. Because the subprime lender owns the property, not the borrower, they are always in the position of benefit.

Whether or not the homeowner was a first-time borrower or refinancing to "get out of debt," accepting a subprime loan to finance a home proved to be too much of a burden for many consumers who quickly found themselves headed for foreclosure. In March 2008, Friedman Billings Ramsey reported the default rate on securitized subprime loans hit 25.2 percent in December 2007. This means that one out of every four homeowners with this type of loan fell into foreclosure.

The Business of Making Money: Banks

Like any company, banks are in business to make a profit. Instead of selling a product from a store shelf, they make money by selling money — YOUR MONEY — in the form of loans, certificates of deposit (CDs) and other financial products. If you visit your local bank to make a deposit into your savings account, the customer at the teller window next to you could be there to borrow money — YOUR MONEY.

The bank has a major advantage over you at this point. They can legally charge and collect interest to lend your money. Banks do pay interest on depositors' accounts, but they charge a higher rate of interest on other products to earn the money to pay that interest. The end result is profit for the bank, even with paying dividends on savings deposited at their institution.[55]

"It doesn't matter how or why you borrowed money, the debt burden and all that goes with it belongs to you."

Recycling Debt

Being a Part of the Problem

If you are in debt, banks and credit card companies are making money off of you. It doesn't matter how or why you borrowed money, the debt burden and all that goes with it belongs to you. At the end of a lifetime of debt, you may have nothing but the lint in your pockets— no money left for emergencies or retirement.

With all the fees, interest, and other costs of borrowing, the consumer rarely gains anything tangible. Especially in the case of mortgages, refinancing simply starts the interest clock all over again — costing the consumer thousands of dollars. Refinancing can create a situation where the consumer never owns their home outright. Even at death, they owe money on a home they've lived in for decades. Is there any cure for runaway debt?

John Washenko and Skyler Witman, co-founders of industry-leading, debt-reduction software, who started their careers in the mortgage industry, witnessed firsthand the tide of the debt epidemic during their tenure as mortgage brokers.

"Clients would return a year or two after we'd set them up with a mortgage begging us to help them again. They'd be totally frazzled and were willing to sign anything to get money back into their budget," Washenko said. "Then, a year or two later they'd come back again wanting another fix to take away their pain. It's like they thought we were money doctors."

Witman adds: "We really had to dole out some tough medicine at times. Saying 'no' to these people was one of the toughest things I've had to do. There was nothing I could do for them anymore. Their financial life seemed like it was over."

Money Momentum

CHAPTER EIGHT
8
CHAPTER EIGHT

THE OVERLOAD OF FINANCIAL ADVICE

"We had 'em [credit cards] maxed out in less than six weeks. Between the car and all these problems, our income was going nowhere but to make the minimum payments."

—Jake H.
Minneapolis, Minn.

While personal finances influence practically every aspect of your life, no one said managing your money was simple. Tracking balances and spending from multiple bank accounts, savings accounts, retirement accounts, investments accounts and loans can be daunting at best. The trick is finding tools that make sense for you and your unique situation. Sounds easy, right? Wrong!

Just walk into your local bookstore or get online for a quick Internet search for personal finance. The results are staggering. For example, by entering the search term "money" on Amazon.com, you'll get nearly 80,000 results. A search for "budget" yields almost 37,000 hits and the term "personal finance" leaves you with approximately 25,000 choices.

So, why are there so many options? What's even scarier than the amount of search results is that not all of the authors that penned these personal finance books are qualified to write on this subject in the first place. Many of these authors are simply writing a book to try and improve their own financial lives.

This situation also spans to financial advice distributed through different forms of media (e.g., radio and television hosts, newspaper advice columnists, etc.). Even if their advice is sound, it might not work for every single person in every type of financial situation. Since communication is a two-way street, what options do you have taking financial advice from these people? Remember, their advice could affect the rest of your life. Can you call the author at home? How long are you going to sit on hold during a radio show to MAYBE get on the air to get your question answered? And considering the barrage of "letters to the editor" the average newspaper or magazine receives, the chances of your questions being read, let alone answered, are extremely slim.

What's missing here is having a coach to guide you every step of the way. Let's say a child has signed up for little league baseball, but the coach stops training after the first practice. How effective is that child going to be during his first game? Probably not very good at all! Without a coach to catch mistakes, answer questions, and put him back on track, that child has little to no chance of reaching success. Same goes for finances — without a coach your chances of making the right fiscal choices at the right time are extremely small.

In fact, statistically the chances of obtaining a net worth of $1 million or more are quite slim. There are close to 6.7 billion people on the planet. According to a 2006 study, there are 8.7 million millionaires in the world who own $33.3 trillion in assets. In a league of their own are the Warren Buffets of the world who are categorized as the extremely wealthy. These individuals boast an incredible net worth of $30 billion or more. Obviously, this category of high-income earners is significantly smaller. Only 85,400 people are considered to be wealthy by this high standard. Nearly half of the extremely wealthy reside in North America.[56]

Paralysis from Fear

Another reason for so many personal finance and money management books is fear. That's right, FEAR. Statistics show that the average adult spends 80 percent of their time earning, spending or thinking about personal finances.[57] Americans are routinely moving toward longer and longer work weeks. Approximately 31 percent of college-educated men work more than 50 hours per week. That figure is up 22 percent from a study conducted in 1980.[58]

Now, factor in all of the time you spend taking care of household bills and expenses, working on budgets, monitoring investments, etc. Also consider the time you spend preparing for work. This includes getting dressed for work, commuting and dropping off children at school or daycare so you can go to work. Don't forget the time you spend shopping and caring for work appropriate clothing. The vast majority of our lives revolve around work — all so we can earn the almighty dollar!

As a result, we become fearful of managing our own money. We are afraid of making poor financial decisions. So we turn to self-help guides, personal finance books, tapes, lectures, classes, and any other tool we can get our hands on. As an American people, we are looking for the secret

"The vast majority of our lives revolve around work — all so we can earn the almighty dollar! As a result, we become fearful of managing our own money."

The Overload of Financial Advice

to success. We're desperate to find any piece of wisdom that will teach us how to get rich quick, better manage our finances, put our money to work for us or any other tool to make our financial situation better, easier and wealthier. We want to become financial experts.

Contradictions and Opposing Opinions

The problem becomes that all of the books, tapes and seminars give different advice. In an effort to sell more tools, authors look for a new, sexy way to differentiate themselves from the rest of the money experts. They need an exciting tidbit that can be used in all of their marketing. To be fair, some authors sell big ideas that have worked for them in the past. After all, personal finances are exactly that — personal. A tool or piece of advice that works for someone else may not be helpful in your unique financial situation.

To illustrate, consider some of America's most famous personal finance experts. These are all names you have heard on television and radio and you see their faces on billboards. But each expert has their own unique way of managing personal finances. They adamantly proclaim their way is the best way a consumer can successfully build personal wealth. But some experts promote a different and sometimes contradicting way.

There is some great advice out there about finances over the radio, television and other media outlets. But one of the biggest stumbling stones for consumers is that each of their circumstances can be quite different. In other words, their personal financial challenges are "customized" to their own daily changing circumstances. Where one expert's advice may be helpful for one person, it may actually cause damage to the next person. And because the mass population cannot reach out and talk with these financial experts, they are caught in a constant financial guessing game.

Your Choice to Change

As a consumer, it's your responsibility to sort through all of the propaganda, marketing strategies and advertising hype to find the true diamonds. These useful tidbits of information will allow you to successfully navigate your finances. But in some situations, the process leads to paralysis. Because the media and various marketing literature promote so many different ways to budget, reduce debt, invest and save money, many people are afraid they will do the wrong thing. They worry they will put their money in the wrong type of account or they will purchase the wrong stock so they simply do nothing. There are too many choices which instill the possibility of making too many mistakes.

In *The Paradox of Choice: Why More is Less*, author Barry Schwartz explains a very interesting phenomenon showing the paralysis people experience when forced to make decisions about their money. One study found that as companies provide their employees with more mutual funds in a 401(k) plan, the chances that employees enroll for the plan goes down. In fact, for every 10 funds added to the plan's option, the employees' rate of participation drops by 2 percent. Increased options even influence employees who do want to take part in the plan. Among investing employees, more options increase the chances that employees will invest in conservative money-market funds instead of more profitable stocks.[59]

In reality, the most important thing you can do is take at least some action toward changing your personal finances. You don't have to be an

> *"Personal finance is a confusing mess of overblown hype, myths and outright deception — and us, feeling guilty about not doing enough or not doing it right."* [60]
>
> —Ramit Sethi, author of *I Will Teach You To Be Rich*

expert, the actions you take don't have to be perfect and you don't have to do everything RIGHT NOW! All you need to do is take one step toward improving your personal finances. Getting started and making a change, no matter how small, is more important than becoming a financial expert even before you get started.

THE PHYSICS OF MOMENTUM

"I felt gullible and lied to but it didn't matter, we still owed the money."

—Kiri H.
Minneapolis, Minn.

Many of you haven't thought about momentum since high school physics, but momentum plays a critical role in your finances. To explain, consider these scientific explanations of momentum. Originally, ancient scientists believed that momentum was not a motion. Instead they thought that the moving object contained powers within itself that allowed it to move.[61]

Today, scientists understand momentum very differently. Simplified, momentum is defined as an object in motion. In scientific terms, momentum is usually expressed with the symbol p. An object with momentum has both a size and a direction. Momentum is equal to the mass of the object multiplied by the object's velocity (p=mv).

Some confuse momentum and velocity. While the two forces are related, they are not the same. Momentum has both mass and velocity. The direction of the momentum follows the direction of the object's velocity. Think about a water balloon thrown at 40 mph and a pickup truck travelling down the road at the same speed. Both have the same velocity, but very different masses and thus momentum. Which would you rather have hit you?

Scientists say that momentum is a conserved quantity. In other words, if there are several items with momentum within a closed system, the total momentum of the system does not change over time. These items may interact with each other and transfer momentum, changing the momentum of the individual objects. But the system as a whole will not lose momentum. This single factor allows scientists to calculate and predict exactly how momentum can transfer among objects.

It is important to consider how outside forces act upon the objects within the system because these forces can alter the momentum of a system. Just consider the forces of gravity. According to the laws of momentum, a ball put into motion would continue to roll in a straight line forever. However, outside forces of gravity and friction cause the ball to slow and eventually stop.[62]

Money Momentum

The laws of physics say that unless an object is acted upon by an outside force, its momentum will allow it to continue to move along at the same speed and in the same direction infinitely. Personal finances operate under the same laws, with either positive or negative consequences.

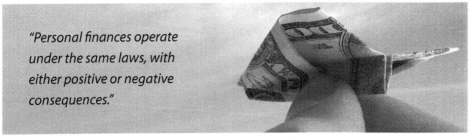

"Personal finances operate under the same laws, with either positive or negative consequences."

Money Momentum

With record high levels of debt, most Americans have negative money momentum. But because America is one of the wealthiest countries in the world, many people enjoy positive money momentum as well. A study conducted in 2006 showed that the majority of worldwide millionaires reside in the North America. That's approximately 2.9 million millionaires.[63]

Negative Money Momentum

If you are one of the millions of American families with consumer debt, you have negative money momentum. Each month, you are required to make a payment on your credit card, department store card, medical bills and other consumer-related debt. Yet, because of high interest rates and the fact that nearly 60 percent of consumers don't pay their credit cards balances in full each month, it's difficult to lower the total amount due.[64]

Paying the minimum amount due on a credit card each month covers interest, any late fees and a typically 1–4 percent of the principal balance. Even if you don't make any additional purchases on the credit card, your bill will come the following month with a similar payment and total amount due. While you continue to make payments each month, you aren't paying down the debt very much at all. You're mainly only paying interest. You are in financial bondage.

Because you are constantly required to make payments to your debts, it is difficult to get ahead by saving money for a rainy day, investing, creating college funds for your children or funding a retirement account for yourself. When you receive additional funds through side jobs, gifts, bonuses, etc., you need to use the money to pay down your debts. Many people with negative money momentum simply loosen their spending belt a bit and the funds seem to magically disappear. No new furniture. No luxurious vacation. No robust savings account. All they have to show for their income is a growing credit card balance. The careful management of funds is non-existent and the negative cycle continues.

The Physics of Momentum

The Cycle of Spending

Unfortunately, negative money momentum also extends to your children. While you carry the burden of constant debt, it becomes very difficult to save up for a college education for your children. We all know the importance of getting a college education because of how dramatically higher education influences earning power. You want your child to be able to provide a nice living for themselves and their future family, so you encourage your child to attend college. However, because you paid the minimum payment on your credit cards for years, you were in financial bondage and were not able to save a single dollar.

Negative money momentum limits your ability to save for your child's college education so your daughter turns to student loans. On average, a college student graduates with $23,186 in student loan debt and $4,100 in credit card debt.[65] In many situations, especially if your daughter attends an expensive private university, she will walk away from school with debt greater than her starting annual salary.

These large loans become particularly burdensome for your daughter as she tries to find her way in the world. With college now behind her, she'll start looking for a first home or apartment and will probably be looking to get married and start a family. She will attempt to do all this with the low earnings from her longed for "first job" and a devastating debt load.

> *Are you teaching skills that promote positive money momentum or negative money momentum?*

Money Momentum

"Paying the minimum amount due on a credit card each month covers interest, any late fees and a typically 1–4 percent of the principal balance."

This negative money momentum is likely to affect her marriage as well. It is well-known that finances are cited as the number one cause of divorce. But bringing debt into a marriage, even student loans, makes the statistical chances of divorce even higher. Because of your poor financial management, you have transferred your negative money momentum onto your child. Now, saddled with excessive debt, she will start her adult/married/career life with negative money pushing against her, too. Statistically, the chances of failing in her marriage and career are very high.

Keep in mind that your child will learn money management skills from you during their entire childhood. For example, you have been teaching your child money management skills since she was a toddler when buying an extra treat at the gas station or as an elementary school child listening to her parents talk about finances at the dinner table. When she reached her teen years, she finally had access to her own money (even if it is yours) and began making her own spending decisions.

Most children and young adults report that they learned their financial management skills from their parents. In fact, 86 percent of teenagers report that they rely on their parents for financial knowledge.[66] If you have been wasteful or excessive with money while raising your child, you are passing those same traits along to her.

"To gain 40 lbs. in 10 years, consume an extra 35 calories every day."

The Little Things: Two French Fries Could Mean 40 lbs.

We've all heard it before — little choices can have a big impact over time, especially with your finances. If you start contributing to your 401(k) in your twenties instead of later in life, you'll acquire hundreds of thousands of extra dollars by the time you retire. Adding $100 in principal to your mortgage payment every month will dramatically shorten the life of your loan and save you potentially tens of thousands of dollars in interest.

The cost of lattes or lunches can dramatically affect your bottom line. In fact, you can save $112,000 over a lifetime by bringing your lunch to work.[67] That drive-thru lunch might not seem expensive at the time, but chances are consumers with substantial credit card debt didn't make one huge purchase. Instead, they racked up the balances by making dozens of smaller purchases.

Each of these seemingly insignificant daily choices about our spending makes a striking difference over the course of a lifetime. Most likely, if you were able to see the end result of your little purchases in advance, you probably wouldn't have made them. We call this: "Financial Foresight." In this regard, personal finances are similar to dieting. All too often, dieters justify "cheating" on their diet. After all, it's just one tiny slice of cake, a handful of chips or a few extra french fries. Two french fries really can't make or break your diet, can it?

Money Momentum

Consider this:

- If you put on 40 pounds over 10 years, you'll gain an average of 4 lbs. per year.
- **1 lb. = 3,500 calories**
- To gain 40 lbs. in 10 years, consume an extra 35 calories every day.
- **35 calories = two regular french fries**[68]

Seemingly insignificant things can and will make a dramatic difference in the long haul.

Money Flow

Wealth flows in and out of our lives. Did you know that approximately 34.5 cents of every dollar that the typical American family earns is spent on interest for debt payments? Most people do not understand that their largest financing needs — mortgages, auto purchases and education loans — will far exceed any other need that they have during their lifetime. Notice how this sounds contrary to what most people consider to be their largest financial need — retirement income. Ironically, the largest culprit of under-funded retirement income is the liability of interest payments flowing away from them during their working years.

Mortgage financing can front-load upwards of 90 percent of your early payments to interest. Interest-only loans apply your entire payment to interest without reducing your principal balance one dime. Auto financing, on average, soaks up 20–25 percent of every payment. A second car, the family boat or high interest credit cards only exacerbate the issue. Combine the obligation to pay taxes and the common goal of setting aside 10 percent for savings or retirement, and there's not much left over for living. Paying interest is the silent killer of your future hopes and dreams.

Banks have thrived for centuries off the fruits of lending. Banks do not invest — they lend! For some unknown reason, the simple idea of making a profit on an interest rate spread seems too challenging for the masses to accept.

So to you we pose this question: What if you could recapture a large amount of the interest and principal that is currently flowing out of your life? How different would your finances look if you were receiving 34.5 percent of your income from your own loans instead of paying out 34.5 percent of your income?

Positive Money Momentum

Now consider the benefits of positive money momentum. When you are wise with your money, you are free to make your own financial decisions. You are no longer pushed along a pre-determined path by the bank, lenders or any other of your financial responsibilities. By making the choice to become debt free, you are able to create an external force that can change the direction of your financial momentum. But, without a plan and a coach the path to overcome the burdens of debt is a long, uphill battle. You must create positive money momentum in your life!

Imagine what your life would be like if you could pay all of your bills on time, lived free of debts, had a hefty savings account to take care of unexpected expenses and had your money working for you to provide for your financial future. You would have excellent credit (or at least you would be creating positive momentum to repair a damaged credit score). Your improved FICO credit score could be helping you save tens, if not hundreds of thousands of dollars of interest on your debts. Because you have been wise with your finances, those debts would only be your mortgage or any loans you strategically choose to take out to expand your personal life or business.

Financial stability allows you to buy exactly what you need, when you need it, greatly eliminating stress from your life. For example, that broken garage door or leaking roof will no longer be a financial disaster. Simply remove the funds from your savings account and move forward. No more credit card debt or home equity loans to keep you in financial captivity.

Money sitting in the bank will also afford you the opportunity to help others during times of need, generating greater personal fulfillment and satisfaction in life. Simply put, positive money momentum gives you the freedom to do more — more family vacations, more free time and more stability. It's peace of mind like you have never experienced before.

Now that you've learned what the benefits are to achieving true financial freedom, the first thing you should ask yourself is, "How do I achieve financial freedom for myself and my family?"

Your Personal Money Momentum

The forces of nature show that momentum, even in personal finances, will continue in the same direction unless acted upon by an outside force. In many cases, that outside force is a dramatic life event such as a medical emergency, a job loss or even a bankruptcy. These extreme life events make people re-evaluate their spending habits and their overall financial situation. Serious self-reflection is required. The question then becomes what corrective actions will be taken? Many people with extreme debt immediately turn to bankruptcy. In many situations, bankruptcy is not the answer. Debt consolidation through a signature loan or mortgage refinance can potentially make your situation even worse.

In both cases, individuals feel like their financial lives are in ruin so they take dramatic measures to avoid, reduce or eliminate monthly payments. However, these so-called "quick fixes" eliminate debt without forcing the consumer to change their spending habits. Many Americans who chose to make these financial decisions often find themselves in the exact same situation a few years (or even months) later. Why? They never made the changes required to slow down or eliminate their negative money momentum to turn their financial situation around and reap the rewards of positive money momentum.

Now take a moment to honestly examine your personal finances. Do you have positive money momentum or negative money momentum? Are you required to pour your financial resources into debt repayment each and every month? If you have debt from credit cards, student loans, medical bills or car payments, chances are you have negative money momentum.

It's time to reverse the flow of your finances. Now is the time to make your finances work for you and generate positive money momentum. With the system on your side, you can do it! Our tools were designed with you in mind so you can find success in your personal finances, gain control of your personal finances and gain positive money momentum!

The next natural question is: "What is the best plan for me to gain positive money momentum?"

DEBT REDUCTION STRATEGIES

"You'd think I would have learned from my parents' mistake. They never planned for the future. Sadly, on my very first day of retirement I was completely broke."

—Herb F.
Portage, Ind.

Let's take a look at some of the debt-reduction strategies on the market today. Some are more effective than others. Listed below are some of the more common types:

Debt Roll Down

You've probably heard of this technique before. Some money experts call this debt-reduction plan the "Debt Snowball Effect." Here's how it works.

Make a list of all your debts. Many experts say you should list your debts according to the highest interest rate first while others say the list should be ranked according to the lowest amount due.

For this section, we will use the approach of listing your highest interest rate debts first on down to your lowest interest rate debts last. Now, make a second column showing the minimum monthly payment for each debt. This should be the minimum amount you are currently paying on the debt each month.

Do everything you can to pay more than the minimum amount on the first debt. This may mean some lifestyle changes on your part, including eliminating unnecessary expenses and potentially having to increase your income. After the first debt is paid off, take the minimum monthly amount of the first debt and apply it to the minimum payment due for the second debt. Then, pay more than the minimum amount due on the second debt until it's paid off as well. Keep rolling the minimum payments from debts you pay off onto the next debt until everything you owe is paid off.

It may take some time to pay off the first few debts. However, after you have paid off debts number one and two, you can start applying their minimum monthly payments to the next debt.

While this can be an effective solution to paying off multiple debts, this method only works for people who are very financially disciplined and have several debts in addition to their mortgage. Those with only a mortgage will not find help in using this type of an approach.

Biweekly Payment Method

The concept behind biweekly mortgage payments is actually quite simple. Instead of making 12 monthly payments on your mortgage each year, your monthly payment is divided in half and withdrawn every two weeks. Because there are 52 weeks in a year, that equals 26 biweekly withdrawals, which equates to 13 full payments per year.

The bottom line to the biweekly concept is that you are making one extra payment to your mortgage each year. This can help to pay 30 year mortgages off an average of 6–7 years early.

STANDARD 30 YEAR EXAMPLE	BIWEEKLY EXAMPLE
$200,000 Mortgage	$200,000 Mortgage
6% Interest	6% Interest
$1199.10 Monthly Payment	$599.55 Biweekly Payment
Payoff Time 30 Years	Payoff Time 24 Years
Total Interest Paid $231,676.38	Total Interest Paid $180,392.78

(Results available on www.bankrate.com)

The result of a biweekly schedule under this loan scenario (if followed exactly) is an interest savings of $51,283.60, and a six year faster payoff schedule. A biweekly payment plan does take discipline and a commitment to stay on track.

Extra Principal Payments

Making extra principal payments is one of the most common options used to help pay down debt and save interest. Paying extra principal has collectively saved consumers billions of dollars in scheduled interest charges.

While this well-known option is used frequently among consumers looking to get out of debt, it has proven to be a challenge to stick to for many people with changing financial circumstances. Here is an example:

Kathy just took out a loan on a new home for $200,000 and decides that she wants to get her mortgage paid off ahead of her 30-year schedule. The interest rate is 6 percent and her monthly payment is $1,199.10. Kathy's current payment schedule has her paying $231,676.38 in interest in addition to her $200,000 principal loan amount.

Kathy is a disciplined person and has set aside an extra $100 that she can pay along with her mortgage payment every month. By adding an extra

$100 to her principal payment, Kathy should be able to pay her 30 year mortgage off in 24.7 years, and save $49,138.87 in interest.

All of this looks great but there are setbacks to paying extra principal. No matter how great the intention of homeowners to pay extra principal toward their loan balance every month, life's unexpected expenses can topple these plans with ease. It becomes too much of a challenge to keep paying that extra money and many people simply give up.

In Kathy's case, her transmission went out. That's an extra $1,900 she wasn't planning on. Then 10 months later her washing machine breaks down. There's another $400 she has to find in her budget. And as life goes on, Kathy falls off track of paying the extra $100 toward her mortgage and never seems to get back on track.

While some of these strategies can be effective in concept, managing them and keeping them organized to your greatest possible benefit can be an entirely different story. There are so many changing circumstances that come into our financial lives on a regular basis. Income goes up and income goes down. Debt increases and rarely decreases. Expenses increase and rarely decrease. Plus, interest rates may change, and we haven't even mentioned taxes. Jobs may change or be lost, etc. Because of these constant changes, it can become nearly impossible to establish, manage and stay on track with a single financial solution all the way until you are completely debt free.

All-Inclusive Solution

After years of researching and studying many different financial strategies, we have found that a combination of several key financial strategies are necessary to achieve the most effective path to financial freedom in today's constantly changing world. These strategies are:

Interest Accumulation: Ensures your money is working for you, making you money 24/7, 365 days a year — even while you sleep.

Interest Float: Allows you to use other people's money, including the bank's, for specific periods of time (interest free).

Interest Cancellation: Makes it possible to pay back a fraction of the interest contracted or normally owed on any given debt.

Strategic Payoff: Evaluates every debt and its variables to find some of the fastest ways to zero … your payoff date!

The best part of these strategies is that you don't ever have to be an expert on them or remember them yourself. Each of these strategies has been systematically programmed into a simple to use online software. All you have to do is enter your individual debt obligations into the program, and these four key banking strategies will instantly be put to work for you. This software system not only directs you on the most strategic way to achieve a zero-debt life, but it also adds simplicity and understanding of how to get ahead financially.

These keys are not new inside the world of successful banking systems. But, it is time to put these proven banking keys on **YOUR** side of the equation.

We have captured some of the most profitable strategies of the banking world. We have coupled it with cutting-edge technology and made it turnkey simple for the masses. With over $350 million in debt cancellation to date, the program has quickly assumed one of the top positions in debt elimination.

Unlocking the mystery behind the actual payoff date, paying off debt in as little as half the time or less, and the ability to make the best on-the-fly financial decisions has made this system the ultimate tool in debt elimination.

Debt Reduction Strategies

Expeditiously removing consumer debt requires more than vigilant budget discipline and a spreadsheet. While others talk about debt reduction strategies from the airwaves and publish endless books on the subject with no ability to follow up, this system offers a reliable "in your hand" software and support tool using proven banking strategies.

In the privacy of your own home you can manage your personal finances like a bank. The program's strategies and sophisticated mathematical formulas are embedded in a user friendly, point and click, Web-based interface environment. Nothing to download or install — everything is at your fingertips and easy to use!

With this system, many people are able to get out of debt in half the scheduled time or less, and you don't have to refinance your existing mortgage. You don't have to invest in stocks or bonds. You don't have to earn extra income. You don't have to change your existing living budget. And, you don't have to do it on your own!

Experience With the System: Mary the Mother

Her original mortgage balance at the beginning of getting on the system was $136,058.76 and she had 28 years left of payments. She, like a good chunk of Middle America, had limited resources and limited means. She was paid semimonthly receiving $1,136.49 for each check. Her mortgage payment was $927.08 and she designated her living expenses at about $1,000 per month. When Mary was introduced to the program, she was told that she could have everything, including her mortgage, paid off in 11.9 years — resulting in $89,586 in interest savings.

"The first thing I noticed was how quickly it freed me from financial pressure," Mary said. "The system removed so much pressure." Mary is well on her way to financial freedom.

Money Momentum

Just to recap …

Most plans falter because the consumer doesn't have the support or coaching needed to see them through to the end.

With this system, not only are you provided with one of the most effective debt reduction strategies available, along with a simple "point and click" software tool that guides you with simplicity and ease, but you are also provided with live customer coaching and support. The average consumer spends 10 minutes or less per month using this simple, yet highly effective system.

Take a look at another consumer's experience using the system:

Experience With the System: Dave the Doctor

Some people might think that doctors have so much money that they don't need a system of debt elimination. Absolutely wrong! The more money you have and the more properties you own, the more you can potentially save. A good example of this principle is Dave, who spent years achieving a medical degree. More years were spent building his practice and purchasing a nice home, as well as a vacation home.

Even though Dave has a $70,000 gross monthly income, he also has a lot of debt. His two homes each have a mortgage. He also has one line of credit. His total debt on his mortgages and line of credit is $1.2 million. The overhead at his office includes supplies, rent, utilities and four employees.

These expenses, coupled with his personal expenses, add up to $56,000 a month. That leaves Dave with $14,000 in discretionary money each month. By utilizing the program, Dave would be able to pay off his two 30-year mortgages and his line of credit in six years, saving $1.3 million in interest. That is a significant savings — even for someone who earns a gross income of $840,000 a year.

Debt Reduction Strategies

Make Your Money Work for You

Once you are debt free, your money can start working for you instead of against you. Consider it a remarkable reward for the steps you took to eliminate debt and reverse the momentum of your personal finances. It's easy to see how the rewards of financial freedom far outweigh the obstacle of debt. You will be free to make your own decisions about what you do with your money because you are no longer in financial bondage. In addition, all of the funds you have been using to make debt payments can now be used in more beneficial ways to increase your positive money momentum.

For example:

Say that by using the system, "Mike" could have his entire debt paid off in 10.4 years versus the 30 years remaining he has now. Now, Mike decides that he wants to purchase a rental property. The purchase price is $150,000 and the mortgage payment is $900 per month. He locates a renter that pays him $1,100 per month.

A $200 net from his rental payment may not seem like a lot, but by having his rental property occupied and paying the mortgage on the rental through this system, he could have the rental paid off in around 5.3 years. Not only does he have all of his debt paid off including his rental property, but he also has a rental income stream of $1,100 per month that he didn't have before. And all of this was accomplished in just under 16 years, versus the 30 years that it normally would have taken just to pay off his regular mortgage.

The point is that Mike has financial options now. He is no longer tied to making interest payments. He is now able to have payments made to him. And, he can continue to make decisions that help him to advance financially more and more as time goes on.

Years to Pay Off	Interest Remaining	Interest Saved	
		Potential	Actual
9.0	$65,088.34	$237,397.71	$23,695.15

Action Plan | Budget | Accounts | Reports | Live Chat | Settings | Log Out

Date	From	To	Amount	☐ True Cost
August 2010				Select Month
8/1/2010	Craig	HELOC	$1,300.00	
8/1/2010	HELOC	Phone	$135.00	
8/1/2010	HELOC	1st Mortgage	$1,199.10	
8/5/2010	Julie	HELOC	$1,200.00	
8/15/2010	Craig	HELOC	$1,300.00	
8/15/2010	HELOC	Food & Dining	$415.00	
8/20/2010	Julie	HELOC	$1,200.00	
8/20/2010	HELOC	Auto Loan	$460.41	
8/30/2010	HELOC	Un-itemized Budget	$1,800.00	
September 2010				Select Month
9/1/2010	Craig	HELOC	$1,300.00	

Add New Action

Accounts Overview
All Accounts History

Budget Overview

Peace of Mind

Another example of positive money momentum is the ability to generate an emergency fund. A savings account is very important because it seems that one of the greatest obstacles to financial independence is life itself. The only thing you can really count on is the fact that there will always be unexpected expenses — a broken clothes washer, a trip to the emergency room or a leaking radiator in your car. No matter how well you try to plan, there are always situations in life that unexpectedly cost significant amounts of money. We call these things life. The best thing you can do to prepare for these inevitable emergencies is create a rainy day fund.

America's Great Recession has generated a renewed interest in building an emergency fund. In February 2009, nearly 15 million people were

Debt Reduction Strategies

out of work, representing a 10 percent unemployment rate.[69] In this economy, you never know when you could be the next one to be downsized or downright fired. Unfortunately, the days of job stability are over. It doesn't matter how good you are at your job. Corporations can't afford to keep underproducing divisions or departments on the payroll. Again, the best thing you can do is plan for the unexpected by generating a savings account.

It's clear that savings rates aren't nearly high enough. Some studies show that savings rates are as low as 1.5 percent and less.[65] Obviously, those numbers won't keep a roof over your family's head during periods of unemployment or underemployment. To be financially stable, you have to have some money stashed away for those unexpected life events.

Now consider what would happen if you put an average car payment of $378 into a savings account every month. You would have just over $9,000 in the bank in 24 months. While that figure wouldn't keep you safe indefinitely, it will keep creditors away until you can get back on your feet in an emergency. But the best part is that nothing brings peace of mind like money waiting to take care of you and your family during times of crisis.

➢ For additional information on this life-changing program, be sure to call the number located on the last page of this book.

Money Momentum

11

GETTING ON THE RIGHT SIDE OF DEBT

"I thought I was invincible. I used to brag to Terri [wife] that we weren't falling victim to buying the latest and greatest gadget every time a new model came out. But in fact we were still financial puppets."

—Mark R.
Seattle, Wash.

The first step is removing the burden of debt as quickly and as simply as possible. Our system levels the playing field by positioning your current situation in harmony with proven banking strategies.

Whether managing your finances or any other aspect of your life, it is very difficult to maintain a clear perspective of your future. Without a well-defined, clear path to achieving any goal, the most focused person will wander nearsightedly into avoidable pitfalls of debt and regret. Making the right decisions become next to impossible when we can't see a clear path to the finish. To make matters worse, we can look back on our missteps with surprising clarity — the curse of "20/20 Hindsight."

But what if you could have 20/20 Financial Foresight? How much further ahead could you be if you knew beforehand the impact of all your financial decisions?

Getting On The Right Side of Debt

Having 20/20 Financial Foresight — imagine the possibilities!

For centuries, banks have used certain core strategies to make YOUR MONEY work for them.

Turn the tide in your favor by making your money work for you instead of against you! You can do exactly that using our system because it measures your financial acuity and maps out some of the quickest paths to becoming debt free, with simplicity and ease.

Financial Empowerment

You must be asking, "How does this work?" Simple really. Making more than you spend each month is a good start. After entering your financial information, the program shadows your life with the ability to adapt to your evolving situations.

Feeding the program with real-time scenarios provides you that personalized glimpse of financial foresight that empowers you to make smart money decisions.

Should I buy that new car?

What is the True Cost of this new boat?

Where should I apply my next bonus?

12

20/20 FINANCIAL FORESIGHT

"There were several days where I didn't think things could get any worse, and then something else would happen. To say that I was stressed out would be putting it too nicely. Sometimes I wonder how I survived it all."

—Rhonda L.
Dallas, Texas

Perhaps the most powerful aspect of the program is the diversity and range of clients that use and benefit from the program. The young couple, the struggling single mother and the wealthy doctor are all able to achieve life-changing results.

Robert & Kathy

To illustrate, let's take a look at Robert and Kathy, who have a simple 30-year mortgage. Without the program they would have paid a total of $231,677 in interest on their $200,000 loan. With the program, they are on track to pay off their 30-year $200,000 mortgage at 6 percent interest in only 9.5 years. Doing the mathematical calculations shows they'll save $158,939 in interest.

Changes to a family's financial picture may happen quite frequently — job changes, pay raises and expenses can all have an impact. Let's say that Kathy changed employers and subsequently received a pay increase through a promotion. She currently brings home approximately $1,200 on a semimonthly basis. That means she receives 24 paychecks per year. At her new job with the promotion, she will receive an increase of $15.18 per paycheck, and she will be paid every other Friday (biweekly). Being paid biweekly means she will receive 26 paychecks a year versus 24 paychecks semimonthly from her old job. Through the software she decides to apply those two extra paychecks per year and the increase of $15.18 per paycheck to their discretionary income.

By making the necessary changes to update their financial situation using the program, the dashboard now reports their years to payoff have decreased from 9.5 to 8.5 and their interest remaining has dropped from almost $73,000 to just over $64,000. Who would have thought a small change like this — two extra paychecks and an additional $15.18 per paycheck — would have resulted in more than a year's worth of payments being removed from the equation as well as almost $9,000 of future interest savings? This dynamic, continually updating reporting in the system allows users to instantly see how their good — and not so good — financial decisions will affect their overall financial picture.

Not every change in their financial picture will take them closer to their payoff goal. Life happens. What if Robert's car completely breaks down and they need to replace it? They decide on a modest $12,000 car and finance it for five years at 5 percent interest. It is easy to add that extra loan into the program. Upon saving the changes, the program will readjust its payoff strategy and calculations to include that loan. Their new payoff time will now be 9.08 years versus 8.5.

You've read that the program is easy to use, but it is educational as well. One of the educational tools is the True Cost feature. The true cost of an item represents not only the original purchase price, but the anticipated interest that could have been saved had that money been utilized to offset the debts entered into the software. That extra cell phone payment is only $135, but the true cost is displayed as $229.11. There is a difference of $94.11. This difference is the potential interest savings Robert and Kathy could achieve by applying the $135 to their program, instead of the extra cell phone bill. In this way, the True Cost feature is an invaluable tool and can provide a financial wakeup call.

Seeing the true cost for these expenses is interesting, but for instances like utility bills, food and clothing, those costs are unavoidable. The True Cost display is more useful when deciding whether to buy an unnecessary item. For example, Robert and Kathy have been thinking about buying a new television. The one they want is priced at $2,000. They can add that to their program along with the anticipated purchase date. The true cost associated with that TV purchase shows as $3,365.91, and adds time to their payoff. This means that they would lose out on nearly $1,400 in potential interest savings and add three months to their payoff. They can now make the choice to purchase the TV or to wait until later. They are armed with the knowledge of what this purchase would truly cost them as it relates to their payoff date and interest saved.

World-Leading Game Changer

A basketball team trails by 18 points. Their morale is down and the prospect of winning seems bleak. Yet they continued to play hard and give it their all. A couple of back-to-back scoring plays spark an amazing comeback. The momentum gained from two textbook-perfect plays created the confidence necessary to recover — and win. The unthinkable soon became obtainable.

How many times have you felt like you were down 18 points within your own financial game plan? Where the 18-point deficit is measured in years and every new money fad or budget idea you attempt to score with has difficulty triggering that elusive game-changing confidence boost.

For thousands of ecstatic consumers, the program has positively altered their attitudes about winning. Don't just take our word for it — review the testimonials at the end of this book to see what others are saying about the program. They are now winning where they had previously felt defeated!

If we could show you how to drastically reduce the amount of interest you are scheduled to pay on your current debts and at the same time eliminate years off those debts as well, would you take the next step to financial freedom?

DETAILED CLIENT EXPERIENCES

Mark & Terri R.
Seattle, Wash.

Like most newlyweds, Mark and Terri dreamed of moving into their own home immediately after getting hitched. The high school sweethearts had carefully mapped out many parts of their future several years in advance. But their pre-wedding house shopping proved discouraging at best. Even with a down payment gift from Terri's side of the family, deciding on a home that would serve function as well as form wore their collective nerves very thin.

"We hated the houses we could afford and couldn't afford the houses we loved," Mark said. "What's worse, most of the homes we could afford were fixer-uppers or needed the basements finished. I didn't have the extra money or the time to become a home renovator. We needed a livable home right away."

Even at bargain prices in today's housing market, fixer-uppers and basement remodels can drain savings and other sources of income — money they had wanted to set aside to start a family. Plus, both types of repair projects can take years to complete. Not to mention they didn't own the tools or a truck to do the job right.

Shortly before giving up their search and renting for a year, Mark received an unexpected promotion and pay raise where he worked as a software developer.

"It couldn't have come at a better time. The extra money helped us qualify for homes we'd been turned down for in the past," Mark said. "Things were finally coming together."

They purchased a nice four bedroom, two bath, modern Victorian-style home that was in foreclosure.

"The house was only two years old when we bought it and still looked brand new. We got it for a really good price, just under $400,000," Terri said. "We couldn't have been happier."

Because the home wasn't in need of any repairs or renovations, Mark and Terri could focus on work and family life. Two years down the road a second promotion finally put them in a situation they'd been hoping for: Mark making enough money that Terri could quit her position as a receptionist to stay home and raise children.

"I was so excited when he told me how much his raise was because I knew it was enough that I could start having kids," Terri said. "I broke down and cried. It was perfect timing for us as a family."

Mark, who usually errs on the side of caution, sat down with his laptop at the kitchen table with pen and paper to review the family's financial situation.

"I looked at all of our monthly debts and tossed in a couple variables to throw things off. Things like Christmas, a new set of tires for our minivan, and the central air unit going kaput," Mark said. "I didn't see anything we couldn't recover from using our current income."

After taking a deep breath, Terri put in her resignation and nervously watched the time pass during her two week's notice.

"That company had been really good to me. I feared losing my income and I didn't want to say goodbye to the people I worked with," Terri said. "They were like my second family, but they understood my reasons for leaving."

By late summer 2006, they were days away from becoming a family of three. On Sept. 20, they welcomed a baby girl into the world. They named the 6 lbs., 2 oz. newborn: Jessica. After spending nearly $2,000 in baby furniture and other accessories to ensure Jessica wouldn't need anything, Mark and Terri brought their bundle of joy home without missing a financial beat.

Everything remained picture perfect — that is until the "Great Recession" of 2007.

"At first, I didn't think much of the so-called "Great Recession." Every economy has its ups and downs. Kind of like taking one step back and two steps forward," Mark explained. "But when I began noticing friends and business associates getting laid off and struggling financially, I started to worry."

Mark had no idea how close to home the recession would hit. It all started with Terri's parents: Gordon and Sharon. These were the people that gave Mark and Terri a substantial gift — $10,000 — to use as a down payment on their home.

"My father-in-law, Gordon, was let go from his company after 19 years — just days away from retiring. It shocked all of us. They were counting on that retirement money and now it's completely gone."

Gordon and Sharon were forced to move in with Mark and Terri. Terri's parents had no money in savings, and were relying heavily on Gordon's retirement income to "take care" of them far into their retirement years. Although there was plenty of room in their home, it upset both households. Plus, Mark's income now had to pay for everything: food, utilities, gas for four cars, and the list goes on.

"I thought I was prepared but I guess I wasn't," Mark confessed.

A routine meeting at Mark's work brought their world crumbling down even further. Mark and several other programmers received pink slips and were sent to the unemployment line.

"I never planned for this at all. I know that I wasn't the senior man on the totem pole but I was a better worker than they were. It didn't matter, I was considered expendable," Mark said. "I was totally devastated."

Considering there were four people at home counting on Mark to take care of them, the drive home that afternoon was the longest of his life.

"I walked in the door and they knew something was wrong. I tried to hide it but the fear showed in my voice," Mark said. "Within 15 minutes, we were yelling at each other and finger-pointing."

After telling his wife and extended family not to worry and that he'd start job hunting on Monday, Mark walked upstairs to his home office and collapsed into a chair.

"The guilt and confusion about it all gave me a migraine," Mark shared. "I kept looking for someone or something to blame and chose the house as the culprit. If only we'd bought a more reasonable house then we wouldn't be in such a mess."

Mark felt his financial plan had been working very well, "I've seen so many other people struggling. I didn't make the same mistakes they did. Why me?"

Mark then convinced himself that if he needed more money, then he'd borrow it. A trip to his bank brought even worse news than being laid off. They were financially overextended — by a lot.

"We learned that our mortgage shouldn't exceed 28 percent of our gross income and all of our debts combined shouldn't exceed 36 percent. We were much worse than that — 35 percent with our first and second mortgage and over 50 percent with all our debts. I was confused on how it all happened."

What had happened to their family is all too common — choosing refinancing as a way to get out of debt and falling victim to the "buy now, pay later" marketing ploys that most businesses use.

"I thought I was invincible," Mark said. "I used to brag to Terri that we weren't falling victim to buying the latest and greatest gadget every time a new model came out. But in fact we were still financial puppets. The only ones laughing all the way to the bank are the banks!"

"By this time the holidays were upon us and my wife and I were fighting day and night. I was fighting with my father-in-law. Terri was fighting with her mother," Mark shared. "If that wasn't enough, the late notices started showing up and my phone started ringing from debt collectors. I wanted to scream!"

Mark decided to contact some of the workers that were laid off in the same group as he was. He wanted to see if they had a plan or a "way out" that he hadn't thought of before. One former co-worker had discovered what he referred to as the "pot of gold at the end of the rainbow." Naturally, Mark was skeptical but wanted to hear him out.

"I went to his house to meet with a representative from the company. I had a thousand questions to ask this guy because I needed to find a solution — RIGHT AWAY!"

Although they had virtually no discretionary income at the time, the agent showed them what they needed to do once Mark got working again. After 10 more weeks of job hunting, he landed a programming job just three miles from their house.

"It pays a little bit less than my old job but I was happy to be working again," Mark said. "I know it sounds corny, but the program saved my marriage," Mark smiled. "I've shaved years off my mortgage term, and now have the rest of my finances on track. I finally understand how money works. Thank you!"

Rhonda L.
Dallas, Texas

Although Rhonda is a tough and sassy Texas girl at heart, a short three years ago she was suddenly faced with a future full of uncertainty when her husband of 15 years left the family high and dry without so much as

a goodbye note. This is a scene all too familiar when families are faced with severe financial problems.

"When my husband left, he took his income with him and left me strapped

Money Momentum

with all the bills," Rhonda said. "What's worse, he left me with no way to take care of my kids. I was scared to death."

After recovering from the initial shock of a pending divorce, Rhonda realized her husband had also cleaned out the family checking account. With several debits still outstanding and no cash to replace the lost funds, her account quickly went from a positive balance to a zero balance to a negative balance. Her only remaining source of purchasing power was a Visa card, but a recent cash advance by her husband left the card completely maxed out.

"There were several days where I didn't think things could get any worse, and then something else would happen," Rhonda shared. "To say that I was stressed out would be putting it too nicely. Sometimes I wonder how I survived it all."

With a house payment due less than two weeks away, Rhonda had to think and act quickly. She spent an entire afternoon on the phone calling anyone she could think of asking for help. After pooling the money she'd received from friends and family, Rhonda was able to pay the mortgage, cable and utility bills, and had enough leftover to fill the cupboards and fridge with $200 in groceries. For the first time in days, she was able to catch her breath.

"I was so grateful for the help but I wasn't stupid enough to think it would get me through things in the long run. I needed a job as soon as possible to earn my own money," Rhonda said.

She dropped out of high school during her senior year to spend time with her future husband. He had graduated two years earlier and landed a job at a local mill as a forklift operator and eventually moved up to the position of dock supervisor. For the area, he was earning a good income and Rhonda was more than willing to start her adult life as soon as possible.

"I didn't see the point in my spending several more months in school just to be a stay-at-home mom. I was impatient and just wanted to get away

Detailed Client Experiences

from it all. So, I took a risk that would come back to haunt me," Rhonda confessed. "I look back now and I see that it was a crazy thing to do. But, it seemed like a really good idea at the time."

A trip to the Texas Workforce office provided a second rude awakening for Rhonda. Without a high school diploma her earning potential was very limited. For Rhonda, quitting high school wasn't an issue of low income or family troubles; she chose to leave high school voluntarily. Employers don't care about your personal situation — they want educated, trained and experienced workers. Rhonda didn't fit any of those categories.

"The few places they were sending me to apply for jobs didn't pay enough money to even survive. Even working two shifts wouldn't have given me enough to pay all my bills and take care of my kids," Rhonda said. "On top of that, I had no experience because I'd been home for 15 years."

After more than three weeks of job hunting, next month's bills starting arriving right on schedule. With her temporary money resources all dried up and nothing in her pockets, Rhonda contemplated surrendering the house to the bank and moving in with an uncle in Ft. Worth. She'd reached a low point in her life where the fight to become debt free was wearing her out. The kids began to ask questions and notice things were never going to be the same.

"I had put so much effort into surviving this ordeal, but nothing ever seemed to come of it," she said. "I wish I'd been more prepared for something like this. Even a few hundred dollars in the bank would have changed my entire situation when this all started," she added.

Her luck would finally change in the form of a clerical position that needed someone to not only start immediately, but they would provide any necessary training. The only drawback was she'd be working the graveyard shift. "I haven't stayed up all night since I was much younger," Rhonda laughed.

Money Momentum

"But, they pay an additional 50 cents for the shift differential and that comes out to an extra $40 bucks per payday. I needed the job badly and every penny I could get my hands on."

Within a month of being on the job, Rhonda enrolled in a GED course through the Texas Department of Adult Basic Education.

"A lot of stuff in these classes came back to me pretty easily. The only class I had trouble with was science," Rhonda smiled. "But then again, I had trouble with science back in high school."

Even with her education back on track and money coming into the household for the first time in nearly three months, things still weren't improving. Bills were being skipped, collection notices were arriving in the mail, and stress levels were higher than ever. Plus, the kids were missing their mom.

Deciding which bill to pay and which bill to pass over for the month is a scary trend that is a key sign to money mismanagement. Without a monthly budget, Rhonda had been trying to pay whatever bill showed up in the mail that day. If she didn't have the money when the bill arrived to pay the minimum payment, she'd set the bill aside for another payday — a fiscally dangerous way to manage your personal finances.

"I work my fingers to the bone, I'm going to school, and I try really hard to find time to spend with my kids," Rhonda shared. "But after all my extra effort, I wasn't any better off than I was before. I was in debt up to my neck and drowning."

At this point, it was only a matter of time before Rhonda and her kids would face foreclosure or bankruptcy. Part of the problem was that she was never taught how to handle money to ensure they had a nest egg for emergencies. When Rhonda was her kids' age, her father would sneak her $20 now and then to spend on whatever her heart desired. She wasn't taught budgeting or saving, and was never made accountable for her purchases.

"After all I had been through; I wanted to keep fighting on my own. I kept thinking that I had gotten this far by pulling up my own boot straps, and that I'd see it to the end," Rhonda said. "It took a lot for me to step back and ask for help with my money problems."

The financial help that Rhonda is talking about is not borrowing money from family again or buying a flat-panel TV on the "buy it now, pay for it later" plan. Instead, she confided in a co-worker about her dire situation and discovered that she wasn't alone.

"I work with a woman that was on her last dime when she and her husband started on the program," Rhonda said. "She told me it took a slight adjustment in her thinking to follow at first because of old habits, but now they don't think about it and let the program do its thing."

Its "thing" is helping people get out of debt.

"I was afraid to meet with the guy at first because I was totally embarrassed. So, I had my friend come over for support and she sat through the entire appointment with me," Rhonda shared. "I can now say that it was the best decision I've ever made. It was a godsend that I got on the program."

Rhonda's financial future was finally crystal clear. With the program, she is able to tell you exactly where every penny she earns is being spent.

"Even if I don't have anything to update in the program, I'll open it up just to look at the dashboard again," Rhonda laughed. "I can hardly believe that I'll be totally debt free in eight years! Did you hear me? I said, 'Eight years!'" "I highly encourage anyone to get on this program. It doesn't matter if you hardly have any debt or you owe everyone in town, this program can help you," Rhonda said. "Don't wait another payday, another late notice or another sleepless night … call them right now."

Herb F.
Portage, Ind.

"Most people remember the early '70s as being nothing but hippies, Vietnam, and disco. For me, corn was my family's life back then," Herb

explained. "Corn was big when I was growing up. There were fields as far as the eye could see."

Herb was raised in northern Indiana, which is on the eastern end of the Corn Belt. Farm life was tough but the family farm was successful and he never went without anything. Around the house, finances never really seemed to be a hot topic at the dinner table and money was never discussed with Herb.

"My parents would hush and whisper when I came into the room if they were talking about money," Herb said. "I'd tease them and say, 'You're not talking about money, are you?'"

By the mid-'70s, the family farm was running at peak performance. But Herb's parents were ready to hang up their hats and call it a career. With no retirement money saved, they sold individual parcels of land until there was nothing left but the house. All the implements were sold at auction and the buildings on the property were either torn down or moved.

"It was emotionally draining to see it all go but I didn't want to farm the rest of my life. I had other ambitions and plans that I wanted to explore," he explained. "Plus, I was an only child so there weren't any brothers or sisters to pass the farm down to either."

Detailed Client Experiences

Sadly, retirement life for Herb's parents was short-lived. After winning a "Bicentennial America" vacation package from a local travel agency, they were killed in a freeway accident near Boston on their way to visit historic landmarks.

"I think I had mentally prepared myself for their death when it came time for each of them to pass away. I wasn't prepared for both of them to go at the same time," Herb shared.

In less than a year, the family farm and his parents were gone. Herb weighed his options and decided that moving back home was best for the long term.

"It was weird moving back into the house with my parents gone and all the land sold," Herb said. "But, this house is bigger and better than the house I owned in Valparaiso."

Because Herb was an only child, he inherited his parent's house which had also served as corporate headquarters and business offices when the family farm was alive and well. After moving back in a month later, Herb focused on his career and renovating his childhood home.

"The house was shaped weird because the front of the house was occupied by the front desk and the accounting people, and then three upstairs bedrooms were made into offices," Herb said. "Plus, there were male and female restrooms. Not many houses have that," he laughed.

Years slipped away from Herb while remodeling his home and living without the fear and worry of a house payment. A retirement nest egg was the farthest thing from his mind.

"Because I had inherited my parent's house when I was in my mid-30s, I never much worried about saving up for retirement," Herb explained. "By the time I hit 65 years old earlier this year, I hadn't had a mortgage for

30 years. But, I also didn't have a dollar to pay for anything now that I'm retired. Sadly, on my very first day of retirement I was completely broke."

Herb's story is shocking but he's not alone. Statistics show that a whopping 43 percent of American workers surveyed had less than $10,000 saved for retirement. A full 27 percent had less than $1,000 put aside in savings. If that wasn't bad enough, the percentage of American workers with virtually no retirement savings at all grew for the third straight year.

"I used to brag to friends that I didn't have a house payment and that life was good," Herb stated. "Who's laughing now?"

For most people, one of their largest financial needs is a mortgage. But, Herb didn't have that problem — he owned his home outright and had for three decades. He also had title in hand for two automobiles and a travel trailer. So, why is he still unprepared for retirement?

"I wasn't rich by any means but I didn't have to fight just to survive like most of my friends and family. I even financed some stuff when I could have paid cash for it," Herb said. "Because I had more discretionary income than the Average Joe, I spent it like there was no tomorrow."

This doesn't include $23,000 in net profit from the sale of his original home. "I spent that money on a trip to San Diego, a dually truck, and a riding lawn mower. I don't even have the truck or the lawn mower anymore," Herb said. "I don't have one tangible item I can hold in my hands that I bought with that money. It just ran through my fingers."

If Herb had put that $23,000 and 30 year's worth of his former house payment ($1,200 a month) in a non-interest bearing coffee can, he would have saved $455,000 for retirement. Now imagine how much of a nest egg he would have grown if he'd chosen fiscally sound retirement options. "You'd think I would have learned from my parents' mistake. They never

Detailed Client Experiences

planned for the future," Herb said. "When they got money from their corn crop sales, they paid bills and bought something. They never put anything away for a rainy day. That's why they had to sell the farmland when they retired."

While talking with friends over coffee one morning, Herb learned about reverse mortgages. The thought of using his house as a retirement piggy bank intrigued him and he set out to learn more about it.

"I almost gave up on it at first because I had to talk to a third-party financial counselor approved by HUD before I could even apply," Herb said. "After that was all over, I filled out the paperwork, got approved, and now I receive a monthly check that I use to pay for my every day expenses."

Reverse mortgages, available to seniors 62 years of age and older, are used to release the home equity in a property as one lump sum or multiple payments. Some homeowners mistake this money as "theirs" when in fact it is a loan. The funds must be paid back, with interest, to the lending institution. The homeowner's obligation to repay the loan is deferred until the owner dies, the property is sold or the owner moves away for 12 consecutive months (e.g., nursing home).

"I had planned on being in my house until I die so this seemed like how my makeshift retirement plan was going to work," Herb said. "I didn't have much of a choice considering I hadn't planned ahead."

Herb was able to be approved for a reverse mortgage with no documentation or proof of income. For reverse mortgages, income and FICO credit score are not considered part of the approval process.

"It is literally more difficult to get a payday loan than a reverse mortgage," Herb laughed.

Combining his reverse mortgage checks with his Social Security retirement benefits, Herb was able to successfully pay all of his debts every month, but had very little discretionary income left over. He was forced to get a job.

"It was the last thing I expected for my retirement — getting a job," he replied. "I wanted to kick back and enjoy life. Instead, I was working 40 hours a week — just like I was before."

With money such an issue at the most important time of his life, Herb started cutting corners hoping that it would help his situation.

"I turned off the cable TV, disconnected my home phone, and reduced the minutes on my cell phone," Herb announced. "Then I called my auto insurance guy to lower the coverage on my truck to just liability."

It was that phone call that changed his situation, not disconnecting and cutting back on life's luxuries.

"He told me he worked at night helping people get out of debt using a software program," Herb said.

Although Herb's situation was nowhere near as bad as many others, he was heading down a path of indebtedness that he hadn't experienced before. He didn't know how to handle the dangers or longtime effects of borrowing and what paying interest can do to your life.

"My life is back on track and even though I still have to work, I have a different view of money and how I spend it," Herb said. "I didn't want to have to think anymore when I retired and the program does my thinking for me. I just enter the information and do what it tells me. It can't get any easier than that," he added.

Jake & Kiri H.
Minneapolis, Minn.

Jake & Kiri sat next to each other during freshman orientation at the University of Minnesota, Twin Cities. They'd never met before and were seated together just by chance. For both of them, it was the first time in their lives they were free to make their own decisions, when to tidy up their dorm room, and what they could spend their money on.

"It was exciting to start making my own choices," Kiri said. "It felt good to not have to listen to a monologue of my dad's advice every time I wanted to buy something that costs more than $20."

"Same here," Jake added. "Back home, my parents insisted on being listed on my checking account and my car title. It's like they didn't trust me."

Athletics were a big part of Jake & Kiri's lives while growing up. Because they were both new to the state of Minnesota and were attending school as student-athletes, they quickly forged a strong friendship. He was attending school on a two-year partial scholarship to play soccer, while she had enrolled with a partial scholarship to play volleyball that was still pending.

"I hope it goes through as I don't have the money to stay here if I get denied," Kiri confessed. "I'd probably have to head back home and attend a junior college instead."

With enough money to only last her freshman year, she hoped her paperwork would get approved after the coaches and school officials watched her play. Jake felt that things were good and would put his financial concerns on the backburner until his junior year rolled around.

Money Momentum

"We knew that thousands of students before us had financially survived their freshman year and eventually graduated." Jake commented. "We knew our situation was not the greatest, so we just hoped for the best and went to class and practice."

But, it didn't take long for the stresses of student life to begin to wear them down. Add in all the time in the gym and specialized training, and you've got two very weary freshmen on your hands. Not to mention the out-of-town games that took them away from their studies and part-time jobs.

"I got a notice from the student affairs office telling me my job at the bowling alley inside the student union building was in jeopardy due to absences," Jake explained. "I showed my supervisor that I was at student-related functions and his response was basically that he didn't care."
Kiri's situation wasn't any better.

"First, I got denied on my partial scholarship and it was devastating. I was counting on that money and the support to pay for school and so I could play volleyball," Kiri said. "They told me to apply again before my sophomore year starts, but that doesn't help me now!"

Along with the freedoms that college life brings, you must also accept fiscal responsibility. Jake and Kiri were beginning to get in way over their heads financially. Due to the loss of Jake's part-time job and Kiri's scholarship denial, they attempted to extinguish every financial situation by using credit. They chose to save their cash for nights out, clothes, and whatever impulse item drew their attention.

After weeks of taxis, city buses, and the on-campus shuttle, they opted to purchase a car together. Sadly, they were convinced by a local "buy here, pay here" dealership that their lack of credit was bound to give them a high interest rate and that they were "lucky" to buy a car at all. By the time they left the lot, Jake and Kiri were more than $30,000 in debt if they made all the payments for the life of the loan.

"The snake also got us for a maintenance plan that didn't seem to cover anything when we brought the car back to get fixed … the NEXT day," Kiri yelled. "The windshield wipers didn't work and neither did one headlight."

Jake explains: "We figured we'd just lick our wounds and admit we had gotten taken. Our only choice at that point was to keep the car and make the minimum payments. That is until we could get rid of it."

Selling the car proved to be extremely difficult — more like impossible. If not only the fact they owed thousands more than the car was worth the moment they left the lot, the college duo discovered they were the third students from the UofM to purchase the same car.

"It was embarrassing," Kiri shared. "Everyone knew the car was junk and that we owed a ton of money on it. I felt gullible and lied to but it didn't matter, we still owed the money."

With their freshman year now well underway, Jake and Kiri were going through a cycle of sleep, eat, study, sports, and then starting all over again the next day. While browsing the cafeteria bulletin board during a study break, Kiri noticed a financial counseling service that was free to students. Like dozens of students before her, she didn't bother to read the fine print.

"It wasn't the counseling part that I was interest in," Kiri smiled. "They were also offering unsecured Visa cards and signature loans up to $5,000. Jake and I needed spending money or our college days were over. I wanted cash and was willing to sign anything to get it."

Jake added: "I convinced myself that there was no difference in borrowing money from these guys than borrowing money from the government

Money Momentum

for student loans. We knew we were treading on thin ice financially, but neither one of us wanted to drop out of school. This was our life now."

While Kiri went home for Christmas break, Jake passed the time drinking in the dorm with his soccer cronies that were also spending the holidays away from home.

"I got stupid and spent $2,000 on stereo equipment to compete in some "loudest music wars" contest on New Year's Eve. It was virtually all the money I had left without the money we got from those loan places Kiri found," Jake said. "What's worse, I had forgotten that a car payment was mixed in with that $2,000."

Because they'd gotten behind on payments before, the lien holder didn't hesitate to collect on their collateral when they'd reached 60 days in arrears. Jake and Kiri's precious form of transportation was repossessed while an audience of over 100 fellow students laughed and jeered as it was hoisted onto the flatbed tow truck.

"It was the most embarrassing moment of my life," Jake confessed. "Even after it was auctioned off, we still owed money on a car we didn't have."

Although their finances were spiraling downward at breakneck speed, Jake and Kiri hadn't seen the worst of it yet.

"Both Jake and I got Visa credit cards with a $2,500 limit from that credit counseling place," she explained. "We had 'em maxed out in less than six weeks. Between the car and all these problems, our income was going nowhere but to make the minimum payments."

Jake added: "And without a car and no way to get another one, we had to go on a waiting list for jobs on campus. I hate to admit it but I was careless with my money — exactly as my parents had predicted."

Detailed Client Experiences

Ironically, Jake and Kiri went back to the financial counseling center to ask for help paying the Visa cards they had issued to them. Instead of lending them more money, the service put the two students on individual budgets.

"The budget was so strict, I couldn't buy anything without having to defend myself," Kiri cried. "I decided to call my parents just like I did when I was a kid."

Calling her parents was the best decision she had made all semester. Her father had recently spoken to a neighbor who had become an agent for a company that helps people get out of debt. The agent explained that he was going to include her finances with her parents. Then, Kiri's father would send a monthly stipend to pay for living expenses outside of school loans, grants, and future athletic scholarships.

"Jake had too much pride to admit he was a financial train wreck and didn't last on the budget but a few days," Kiri said. "Now he's trying to get out of debt on his own. When he runs into trouble, he simply borrows the money from me. But, I can't help him for much longer."

After eight months on the program, 30 percent of the debt that Kiri had racked up in one school year had been paid down. Although she was turned down for a volleyball scholarship twice, she had learned a hard lesson and began making wiser money choices.

"I took a while to get it through my thick head that easy credit quickly turns into chasing interest rates for the rest of your life," Kiri said. "No more debt burdens for me."

➢ For additional information on this life-changing program, be sure to call the number located on the last page of this book.

Money Momentum

CHAPTER FOURTEEN

14

CHAPTER FOURTEEN

THERE HAS TO BE A BETTER WAY

*"The guilt and confusion about it all gave me a migraine.
I kept looking for someone or something to blame and
chose the house as the culprit. If only we'd bought a more
reasonable house then we wouldn't be in such a mess."*

**—Mark R.
Seattle, Wash.**

Barely toddlers when they became friends, no one could have guessed what the future held for Skyler Witman and John Washenko as they grew up together. In some respects, their childhoods mirrored one another as experiences in their nondescript Salt Lake City neighborhood set the stage for a friendship that has travelled from early youth to today's innovative business partners.

In his early teenage years, Witman witnessed real life financial challenges when the family home was repossessed and literally watched a tow truck back into the driveway and take away the family cars. The emotions he felt during this trying time have stuck with him and provide the motivation he needed to develop a solution to the debt problem.

For Washenko, the disastrous effects of foreclosure were also far-reaching. He experienced similar emotions when his father's home was sent into foreclosure.

Washenko remembers, "And when that happened, it [foreclosure] was one of hardest things ever in our family."

Although Witman and Washenko might not have understood exactly how or why finances had burdened their families, they realized there was one common denominator: unmanageable debt. While working together in sales throughout high school, Witman and Washenko got their first taste at managing and working with their own money.

"When Skyler and I were kids, we got a good understanding of finances and how money is hard to come by," Washenko pointed out.

Childhood can be very impressionable and for Witman and Washenko, watching their parents' exhaustive efforts to battle debt and get ahead was not pleasant. That common bond sealed their destiny to help people and to ensure the same thing — unmanageable debt and foreclosure — didn't happen to other families. That bond grew out of foreclosures and other consumer-related hardships and would manifest itself later in life, during the development of one of today's most innovative debt management and wealth building systems.

By the time they entered the business world, the bond formed during youth had not waned. In fact, they had decided to join forces and become business partners.

"Initially we didn't know exactly what we wanted to do, but we knew we wanted to go into business together," Witman said.

That business partnership eventually drew them to working in the mortgage industry — something they could easily relate to firsthand. In 1997, the pair launched their own mortgage company. Their entrepreneurial spirit and unmatched enthusiasm to help homeowners quickly placed them as one of Utah's fastest-growing companies by its third year in business. Their enthusiasm was short-lived as a common thread began to plague the mortgage lending industry.

"After we had completed several mortgages, we realized that setting someone up with a refinance or second mortgage wasn't necessarily helping them to succeed in life," Washenko said. "It didn't help them achieve their financial goals. It just lowered their monthly payment and created more debt."

Witman's sentiments echoed Washenko's: "This kind of went against our goal. We had hoped to help homeowners get into a better situation."

At this point they started to see a pattern of recycling debt when their customers would return years later in a much worse situation than they had been in before.

"After seeing too many homeowners coming back to us, who had dug themselves deeper and deeper into this financial pit, we decided that there had to be a better way," Witman said.

That better way took years of research and development and was based on their personal beliefs to create a better solution.

"While debt is a necessary part of our lives, it's not something that I feel has to control our lives," Witman explains.

So, armed with a dream that everyone should be able to control and eliminate their debt, Witman and Washenko set about to change the way homeowners could take control of their debt — beginning with their mortgages.

They initially decided to offer their clients various debt reduction plans such as biweekly payments, but the results proved unsatisfactory. After five years in the mortgage industry, they began to search for an even better answer and

There Has To Be a Better Way

discovered it in a system that mimics the people who know money better than anyone: banks. They knew that banks "sweep" their customers' accounts at the end of each banking day, and then use that money to their advantage.

So, why couldn't the average consumer do something similar with their own accounts — their own money?

Simple math dictates that the lower the principal amount owed the less interest a homeowner will pay. Essentially, this means using the homeowner's stagnant money located in their checking/savings account to reduce the principal balance owed on their mortgage. But, fine tuning that simple math into a user friendly software program, which would handle mortgages and consumer-related debt, would still be years in the making. Plus, it must conform to U.S. banking regulations.

Recognizing that a complicated and provable mathematical algorithm would need to be developed to meet all of these objectives, Witman and Washenko contracted a high-profile aeronautical engineer to spearhead the technological development. The end result was the prototype of our flagship software. Now it was time to put everything to the test — with real debt and real people.

After a yearlong beta test, which included a 400-client test market in Denver, Colo., the results exceeded their expectations and forecasts. They knew they were onto something … BIG! The results were so impressive that some homeowners reported they were ahead of the predicted payoff time by as much as 20 percent. This was very exciting news!

With the system ready for the general public, Witman and Washenko next sought to find a platform to make their product available to clients. Before they started their consumer distribution platform, Witman and Washenko first needed to forge an alliance with likeminded and experienced mortgage professionals to facilitate the distribution efforts and manage the growing demand for this new program.

Money Momentum

Witman and Washenko brought on business partners Jonathan E. Bonnette and Matthew Lovelady to form the only company utilizing banking strategies in this way to help the ordinary consumer to become debt free.

Final Thoughts

Indebtedness is a dangerous thing. It's like a disease that will continue to cause infection and if not treated will cause financial death. It is extremely easy to allow debt to take over every aspect of your life. It starts out slowly — eating lunch out every day at work to a big screen TV for the big game to a car with every option and then a new house that is 1,200 sq. ft. larger than you need.

Then all of a sudden you realize there is more month left but no more money to get you there. What a horrible feeling! But, you don't have to deal with that anymore because you've taken the first step in realizing there is a problem and are taking the steps to find a solution. Now when you make purchases of any kind you will go beyond "Do I need it or do I want it?" to saying "What is the true cost and end result if I purchase this item?"

The responses we've received from this book have been astounding and far-reaching. Just like when we realized that something big was about to happen during development of the software — you now realize the same thing. Debt does not have to rule your life. From this moment forward, you can be an educated consumer and be in total control of your finances. Yes, you can be debt free!

Jonathan E. Bonnette   Matt Lovelady   John Washenko   Skyler Witman

> For additional information on this life-changing program, be sure to call the number located on the last page of this book.

There Has To Be a Better Way

Sources:

1. Steve Rhode, "The History of Credit and Debt," How to Get Out of Debt (2000-2009), http://getoutofdebt.org/14188/the-history-of-credit-debt-interest (accessed Jan. 13, 2010).

2. L. W. King (translator), "Hammurabi's Code of Laws," Exploring Ancient World Cultures (1997), http://eawc.evansville.edu/anthology/hammurabi.htm (accessed Nov. 10, 2009).

3. "History of Dow Jones Industrial Average," MD Leasing Corp. (2009), http://www.mdleasing.com/djia.htm (accessed Nov. 4, 2009).

4. Jessica Pressler, "What Happened at Lehman, in 30 seconds or less," New York Magazine (2008), http://nymag.com/daily/intel/2008/09/what_happened_at_lehman_in_30.html (accessed Jan. 17, 2009).

5. Kathleen Pender, "Government bailout hits $8.5 trillion," San Francisco Chronicle (2008), http://www.sfgate.com/cgi-bin/article.cgi?f=/c/a/2008/11/26/MNVN14C 8QR. DTL (accessed Jan. 16, 2009).

6. United States Department of Labor. Bureau of Labor Statistics (2010). http://www. bls.gov/web/laus/laumstrk.htm (accessed April 6, 2010).

7. "How Debt Affects Your Health." Minimal. Feb. 8, 2010. http://freeloanfinance.com/ how-debt-affects-your-health (accessed April 21, 2010).

8. Liz Pullium Weston. "Why Credit Counseling Often Fails." MSN Money. http://articles. moneycentral.msn.com/Banking/YourCreditRating/TheConsumersGuideToCredit Counseling.aspx. (accessed March 29, 2010).

9. Stone, Brice and Rosalinda V. Maury. "Indicators of personal finance debt using a multi-disciplinary behavioral model." Science Direct. Feb. 7, 2006. http://www.sciencedirect.com/science?_ob=ArticleURL&_udi=B6V8H-4J6W6X4-1&_ user=10&_coverDate=08%2F31%2F2006&_rdoc=1&_fmt=high&_orig=search&_ sort=d&_docanchor=&view=c&_searchStrId=1301358848&_rerunOrigin=google&_ acct=C000050221&_version=1&_urlVersion=0&_userid=10&md5=d127d180ba689 2994fbb1e7d3a71faee. (accessed April 12, 2010).

10. Anthony Karydakis, "How long will the recession last?" CNN Money: Fortune (2008), http://money.cnn.com/2008/12/03/news/economy/karydakis.recession.fortune/ index.htm (accessed Nov. 3, 2009).

11. *"Finances In the family, specifically how debt affects marital relationships and relates to divorce." Thinking Made Easy. April 23, 2009. http://ivythesis.typepad.com/ term_paper_topics/2009/04/finances-in-the-family-specifically-how-debt-affects- marital-relationships-and-relates-to-divorce.html. (accessed April 15, 2010).*

12. *"Finding." Jan. 2008. http://www.familyfacts.org/findingdetail.cfm?finding=8843 (accessed April 21, 2010).*

13. *"Are you stressed and overspending?" MSN Money. http://moneycentral.msn.com/ content/Savinganddebt/Savemoney/P112490.asp (accessed April 2, 2010).*

14. *ASA Aarons. "Study links debt to low self-esteem." NY Daily News. July 31, 2008. http://www.nydailynews.com/lifestyle/2008/08/01/2008-08-01_study_links_debt_ to_low_selfesteem.html#ixzz0l8yUdpwU (accessed April 13, 2010).*

15. *http://metalib.lib.byu.edu.erl.lib.byu.edu/V/HF5PK3T4UARXICTSD9QEDX- H3JD6DYLB7Y4TCVJJ9BA6RNF874S-00823?func=meta-3&short-format=002&set_ number=014753&set_entry=000008&format=999*

16. *"The top fifteen personal finance statistics that will blow your mind." Own the dollar. Oct. 13, 2009. http://ownthedollar.com/2009/10/top-fifteen-personal-finance-statis- tics-that-will-blow-your-mind/ (accessed April 1, 2010).*

17. *"50+ reasons for money 101: a collection of personal finance statistics." Money 101. http://www.money-101.com/50plusreasons/50-reasons-money-101-collection- personal-finance-statistics (accessed March 22, 2010).*

18. *Getlen, Larry. "Why we lie about money and debt." Bank rate. April 28, 2005. http:// www.bankrate.com/brm/news/financial-literacy2004/debt-psychology.asp (accessed April 7, 2010).*

19. *Lazarony, Lucy. "The psychology of debt: why we do the things we do." Bank rate. Jan. 22, 2002. http://www.bankrate.com/brm/news/cc/19980713a.asp (accessed April 19, 2010).*

20. *"The locus of control." Wikipedia: The free encyclopedia. http://en.wikipedia.org/ wiki/Locus_of_control (accessed April 28, 2010).*

21. *Winerman, Lea. "Maxed out: why some succumb and others steer clear." American Psychological Association. June 2004. http://www.apa.org/monitor/jun04/maxed. aspx (accessed April 11, 2010).*

22. *http://metalib.lib.byu.edu.erl.lib.byu.edu/V/HF5PK3T4UARXICTSD9QEDX- H3JD6DYLB7Y4TCVJJ9BA6RNF874S-00823?func=meta-3&short-format=002&set_ number=014753&set_entry=000008&format=999*

23. Loftus, Mary. "Till debt do us part." Psychology Today. Nov. 1, 2004. http://www.psychologytoday.com/articles/200411/till-debt-do-us-part. (accessed April 14, 2010).

24. "Finances in the family, specifically how debt affects marital relationships and relates to divorce." Thinking Made Easy. April 23, 2009. http://ivythesis.typepad.com/ term_paper_topics/2009/04/finances-in-the-family-specifically-how-debt-affects-marital-relationships-and-relates-to-divorce.html. (accessed April 15, 2010).

25. "A pre-marriage look at how debt affects marriage." Marriage missions international. http://www.marriagemissions.com/how-debt-affects-marriage/ (accessed April 11, 2010).

26. "The cost of debt on your relationships." DebtGoal. Feb. 24, 2009. http://www.debt-goal.com/blog/the-cost-of-debt-on-your-relationships/ (accessed April 2, 2010).

27. Cobb-Clark, Deborah and Ribar, David. "Financial stress, family conflict and youths' successful transition to adult roles." Institute for the Study of Labor. Dec. 2009. http:// ftp.iza.org/dp4618.pdf (accessed April 18, 2010).

28. Whitbeck, Les et. al. "Family economic hardship, parental support and adolescent self esteem." Social Psychology Quarterly. 1991. http://www.jstor.org/pss/2786847 (accessed April 12, 2010)

29. Greenberger, Ellen et. al. "Adolescents who work: effects of part-time employment on family and peer relations." Journal of Youth and Adolescents. Aug. 15, 2005. http:// www.springerlink.com/content/x65654201j8j5614/ (accessed April 24, 2010).

30. "50+ reasons for money 101: a collection of personal finance statistics." Money 101. http://www.money-101.com/50plusreasons/50-reasons-money-101-collection-personal-finance-statistics (accessed March 22, 2010).

31. "Effects of poverty." Children in Wales. http://www.childreninwales.org.uk/areasof work/childpoverty/endchildpovertynetwork/2156/2160/index.html. (accessed April 25, 2010).

32. "Consumer debt: an illness the needs to be treated early says leading economic psychologist." PRNewswire. http://www.prnewswire.co.uk/cgi/news/ release?id=158771 (accessed April 4, 2010).

33. McGonigal, Kelly. "Debt and stress." The Washington Post. July 24, 2007. http://www.washingtonpost.com/wp-dyn/content/discussion/2007/07/23/ DI2007072300775.html (accessed April 26, 2010).

34. Partridge, Stephanie. "Family debt facts." eHow. http://www.ehow.com/ about_5484616_family-debt.html. (accessed April 4, 2010).

35. "How Debt Affects Your Health." Minimal. Feb. 8, 2010. http://freeloanfinance.com/ how-debt-affects-your-health (accessed April 21, 2010).

36. "Debt and your health." Wiley InterScience." http://www3.interscience.wiley.com/ journal/118531321/abstract?CRETRY=1&SRETRY=0 (accessed April 11, 2010).

37. Ehrenreich, Barbara. "Suicide spreads as one solution to the debt crisis." AlterNet. http://www.alternet.org/economy/93077/ (accessed April 20, 2010).

38. "The top fifteen personal finance statistics that will blow your mind." Own the dollar. Oct. 13, 2009. http://ownthedollar.com/2009/10/top-fifteen-personal-finance-statistics-that-will-blow-your-mind/ (accessed April 1, 2010).

39. "50+ reasons for money 101: a collection of personal finance statistics." Money 101. http://www.money-101.com/50plusreasons/50-reasons-money-101-collection-personal-finance-statistics (accessed March 22, 2010).

40. Britton, Daniel. "Scary statistics about students and money." Financial Fairy Tales. Feb. 25, 2010. http://www.thefinancialfairytales.com/blog/2010/02/scary-statistics-about-students-and.html (accessed April 22, 2010).

41. Howard, Diana. "Should the federal government offer foreclosure bailout relief for struggling home owners?" Helium. http://www.helium.com/users/149015/show_articles (accessed April 17, 2010).

42. Cottrell, Hazel. "The psychology of debt." Credit Choices. http://www.creditchoices.co.uk/psychology-of-debt-help.html (accessed April 17, 2010).

43. Feldman, Chris. "Record 2009 foreclosure rate is mixed bag of news." Wallet Pop. Jan. 14, 2010. http://www.walletpop.com/blog/2010/01/14/record-2009-foreclosure-rate-is-mixed-bag/ (accessed April 4, 2010).

44. "Foreclosure activity hits record high in third quarter." Reality Trac. Oct. 15, 2009. http://www.realtytrac.com/foreclosure/foreclosure-rates.html (accessed April 9, 2010).

45. U.S. Courts. Bankruptcy Statistics. "2009 Calendar Year by Chapter." http://www.uscourts.gov/bnkrpctystats/statistics.htm#june (accessed April 9, 2010).

46. *"The top fifteen personal finance statistics that will blow your mind." Own the dollar. Oct. 13, 2009. http://ownthedollar.com/2009/10/top-fifteen-personal-finance-statistics-that-will-blow-your-mind/ (accessed April 1, 2010).*

47. *Pulliam Weston, Liz. "How much should you spend on…" MSN Money. http://articles.moneycentral.msn.com/SavingandDebt/LearnToBudget/how-much-should-you-spend-on.aspx (accessed April 8, 2010).*

48. *"The value of a college education: tuition costs, earning power and unemployment rates." Five Cent Nickle. http://www.fivecentnickel.com/2010/04/02/the-value-of-a-college-education-tuition-costs-earning-power-and-unemployment-rates/ (accessed April 18, 2010).*

49. *"Causes of poverty: education and ability." Notre Dame. www.nd.edu/~jwarlick/documents/C10EducationAbilityF08.ppt (accessed April 18, 2010).*

50. *Nyhan, Paul. "College divide threatens to keep the poor in poverty." Seattle Post. Sept. 27, 2005. http://www.seattlepi.com/local/242389_access27.html (accessed April 18, 2010).*

51. *Brady-Smith, Christy et. al. "Poverty and education: overview, children and adolescents." State University. http://education.stateuniversity.com/pages/2330/Poverty-Education.html (accessed April 18, 2010).*

52. *Hirano, Keiji. "Academic ability, drop out rate, poverty clearly correlate study shows." Japan Today. http://www.japantoday.com/category/lifestyle/view/academic-ability-dropout-rate-poverty-clearly-correlate-study-shows (accessed April 18, 2010).*

53. *M.P. Dunleavey, "The worst kind of debt: Charging the groceries," MSN Money (2006), http://articles.moneycentral.msn.com/SavingandDebt/ManageDebt/TheWorstKindOfDebtChargingTheGroceries.aspx (accessed Nov. 9, 2009).*

54. *"A Consumer's Guide to Mortgage Refinancings," The Federal Reserve Board (2009), http://www.federalreserve.gov/pubs/refinancings/default.htm (accessed Nov. 9, 2009).*

55. *Lee Ann Obringer, "How Banks Work," howstuffworks (2009), http://money.howstuffworks.com/personal-finance/banking/bank4.htm (accessed November 9, 2009).*

56. *WWS. "How many millionaires are there in the world?" Oct. 16, 2006. Worldwide Success. http://ww-success.com/blog/index.php/2006/10/16/millionaires-in-the-world/ (accessed May 2, 2010).*

57. "FInances in the family, specifically how debt affects marital relationships and relates to divorce." Thinking Made Easy. April 23, 2009. http://ivythesis.typepad.com/ term_paper_topics/2009/04/finances-in-the-family-specifically-how-debt-affects-marital-relationships-and-relates-to-divorce.html. (accessed April 15, 2010).

58. Mandel, Michael. "The real reasons why you're working so hard and what you can do about it." BuisnessWeek. Oct. 3, 2005. http://www.businessweek.com/magazine/ content/05_40/b3953601.htm (accessed April 26, 2010).

59. Schartz, Berry. In The Paradox of Choice: Why More is Less. HarperCollins. Publisher Inc. New York: 2004.

60. Sethi, Ramit. I Will Teach You To Be Rich. Thomas Allen and Son Limited. Canada. 2009.

61. "Momentum." Wikipedia: The free encyclopedia. http://en.wikipedia.org/wiki/ Momentum (accessed April 21, 2010).

62. "The definition of momentum." http://id.mind.net/~zona/mstm/physics/ mechanics/momentum/definition/momentumDefinition1.html (accessed April 21, 2010).

63. WWS. "How many millionaires are there in the world?" Oct. 16, 2006. Worldwide Success. http://ww-success.com/blog/index.php/2006/10/16/millionaires-in-the-world/ (accessed May 2, 2010).

64. Getlen, Larry. "Why we lie about money and debt." Bank rate. April 28, 2005. http:// www.bankrate.com/brm/news/financial-literacy2004/debt-psychology.asp (accessed April 7, 2010).

65. "The top fifteen personal finance statistics that will blow your mind." Own the dollar. Oct. 13, 2009. http://ownthedollar.com/2009/10/top-fifteen-personal-finance-statistics-that-will-blow-your-mind/ (accessed April 1, 2010).

66. "50+ reasons for money 101: a collection of personal finance statistics." Money 101. http://www.money-101.com/50plusreasons/50-reasons-money-101-collection-personal-finance-statistics (accessed March 22, 2010).

67. "The top fifteen personal finance statistics that will blow your mind." Own the dollar. Oct. 13, 2009. http://ownthedollar.com/2009/10/top-fifteen-personal-finance-statistics-that-will-blow-your-mind/ (accessed April 1, 2010).

68.   Krueger, David. "French fried, credit card and debt psychology: the behavioral economics of small decisions. Free Money Finance. http://www.freemoneyfinance.com/2010/03/french-fries-credit-cards-and-debt-psychology-the-behavioral-economics-of-small-decisions.html (accessed April 18, 2010).

69.   "ABCs for a great car loan." MSN Money. http://articles.moneycentral.msn.com/SavingandDebt/SaveonaCar/ABCsForAGreatCarLoan.aspx (accessed May 2, 2010).

70.   United States Department of Labor. Bureau of Labor Statistics. "Employment Situation Summary." April 2, 2010. http://www.bls.gov/news.release/empsit.nr0.htm (accessed April 18, 2010).

For additional information on this life-changing program, please call the following number:

877-616-5569

Thank You!